A Taste of Santa Barbara™

CRAFTING A MEAL

by Chef ROBIN GOLDSTEIN

Published by PRIVATE CHEF ROBIN

Copyright © 2016 by Robin Goldstein

Printed in the United States of America
First Printing, 2016
For A Taste of Santa Barbara
ISBN: 978-0-9977813-3-5
Printed through Ingramspark

www.ATasteofSantaBarbara.com
www.ATasteofOjai.com
www.privatechefrobin.com

Designed and produced by Constanza Di Gregorio
www.constanzadigregorio.com
cdigregorio@gmail.com

Photography by Jess Roy and Karen Nedivi
Photo credit page 19: tracysmithstudio.com

Edited by Kamila Storr
Index by Jen Weers

Dedication

For my dad, Ron Goldstein, who drove me to the Culinary
Institute of America in Hyde Park, New York in 1982
and supported my journey as a chef.

I LOVE YOU, DAD!

CONTENTS

Taste of Middle East / 125

INTRODUCTION
CRAFTING A MEAL

It is no coincidence that Santa Barbara is known as the "American Riviera". With its Mediterranean climate and a melting pot of cultural and culinary influences, one could mistake Santa Barbara for France's Cote d'Azur or Italy's Amalfi Coast. Santa Barbara integrates foods, languages and traditions from all over the world. Just like the Mediterranean, Santa Barbara thrives on the spirit of eating local, seasonal ingredients. California's Central Valley has some of the most fertile soil in the world and the many kinds of produce grown here play an important role in our local cuisine, along with our amazing Pacific Coast seafood and the many artisanal hand-crafted products that abound. Each culinary influence adds a key dimension to the whole.

This book is inspired by my incredible, life-changing opportunities of traveling and living in Europe. Trips with friends and visiting many countries on the back roads of Europe in a beat-up 1983 Volkswagen van, the delicious flavors, colors and aromas of the Mediterranean have lingered with me, influencing my personal approach to food. To my delight, I found many of these same flavors and the wonderful connection people have to their food when I moved to Santa Barbara. To share my experiences and the memorable meals from my travels, I have hand picked a few of my favorite dishes from the Mediterranean Coast, featuring dishes from Spain, Provence, France, Tuscany, the Greek Islands, the Middle East and Morocco. These chapters include highlights and themed menus around each country's most prominent flavors, circling back to Santa Barbara, California for an eclectic mesh from faraway lands.

I have been a chef for 34 years now. My interest and passion for this profession began at the age of 14. My career as a chef has allowed and required I be both an artist and a craftsman. I believe I am an artist first, who has poured all my creative energy into my craft in the kitchen, putting in many hours of practice and repetition which is a necessary foundation for success. As part of my personal and professional journey after graduating culinary school, I focused both on my craft and my creativity, while embracing the ability to create a successful business at the same time.

My love of cooking is deep-rooted. I was raised in a restaurant family— my grandparents on both sides owned restaurants, as did my father. At a very young age, I learned how to operate the soda machine, was taught how to make a "Shirley Temple", as well as a perfect omelette and how to plate food for service. Working in the kitchen was instrumental in fostering a love of food and a strong work ethic.

Besides my family, another important influence on my culinary journey was Julia Child, who brought both technique and passion for quality ingredients into everyone's home. I welcomed Julia into mine each day while watching *The French Chef*, her iconic television show. Soaking up her knowledge as I was discovering the love of cooking, Julia's impact on food and cooking still resonates with me. Her clear and concise cooking tips like, "Always read the entire recipe first, even if it is familiar to you", from *Mastering the Art of French Cooking*, and, "To peel a clove of garlic, place the garlic on your work surface, lay the flat side of a large knife on it, and smash it with your fist. The peel is then easy to pick off and discard", from *In Julia's Kitchen With Master Chefs*, helped create my foundation as a future chef. One of my favorite Julia quotes is, "Cooking is like love; it should be entered into with abandon or not at all." I couldn't agree more.

Having an artist as a grandmother gave me a front-row seat to the life of a designer and creator. Not only was my grandma Hilda a very accomplished painter, she was also an incredibly versatile cook. She taught me at a very young age to immerse myself in the creative nature of cooking without recipes, guided by my senses. To feel and taste rather than be a slave to the words on a card. As a private chef and event planner here on the Central Coast, food has become my art form. While painting appeals to our sense of sight, food appeals to ALL five senses at once. The flavors and textures, colors and aromas all play a role in a successful dish. Sharing these home-cook friendly recipes, I strive to offer a variety of tastes with the ethnic influences I have been exposed to during my travels.

One thing is certain: as a cook, my work and life can never be separated. Without a doubt, I have become my career and my profession never leaves my side. I feel very fortunate to be able to practice my craft in Santa Barbara, where the sun is almost always shining, the local ingredients are abundant year-round and the possibilities for creativity are endless.

Chef Robin

SEASONING WITH SPICES AND SALTS

Salt rounds out flavors. By adding salt, you will always elevate the flavors of the other ingredients in your foods. We season, cure, brine, preserve, and pickle with salts. Why not infuse the salts to flavor our dishes, to brighten up and shift the taste ever so slightly? For each recipe in this book, you can refer to these three variations of infused salts as well as the three distinct spice blends to enhance the Mediterranean-influenced dishes. I like to use a different salt or spice depending on either the type of cuisine I am preparing or a flavor I would like to infuse more deeply into the dish. The line "salt to taste", often used in recipes, means to salt to your own preference. Once you learn the tricks of getting the salty and savory tones in balance, you'll be seasoning like a pro.

THE SPICES

Dukkah   Crushed pistachio with toasted sesame seeds, coriander, fennel and cumin with a touch of sea salt to season vegetables or use as an herb crust for fish or chicken.

Harissa   Aleppo pepper with paprika, garlic, and cayenne pepper with a touch of sea salt. Mix harissa spice into ground meats or blend into mayo for a zesty condiment or salad dressing. Mix with olive oil to create your own harissa paste.

Santa Barbara Fiesta   Organic paprika, chili powder, garlic, onion and crushed red chili with a touch of sea salt. With an emphasis on Mexican use on meats, dips and popcorn to enhance the flavor.

THE SALTS

Chile Garlic   Pacific Sea Salt with Paprika, Cumin, Garlic, Onion, Jalapeno and Cayenne. Sprinkle chile-garlic salt blend on practically everything and anything you would put garlic on, shrimp, chicken wings, green beans or spaghetti.

Lemon Rosemary   Pacific Sea Salt with Lemon And Rosemary. Sprinkle over grilled meat, popcorn, homemade potato chips, fish, roasted chicken, roasted vegetables or focaccia. It's super versatile!

Mediterranean   French Grey Sea Salt with Thyme, Lavender, Basil, Marjoram, and Fennel. Use this herbed salt to season everything from grilled pork and salmon to soups, tomato salad, vinaigrettes and sauces.

MAKING THE MOST OF YOUR FARMERS MARKET EXPERIENCE.
HERE ARE A FEW TIPS.

Make a list Write down things you know you will need for the week, thinking through what you may need for breakfasts, lunches, and dinners. Chose a few new recipes to try from what is available in season to buy. There is nothing worse than buying the first strawberries you see at the market, that look perfectly red-ripe and delicious, and then discovering they are not that great … and then, a few stands down you find the most fragrant berries you have ever tasted. Many market vendors offer tastes and sampling is vital, particularly for fruit, as this way you get to compare before you decide. I suggest browsing and walking through the entire market before making your purchases. Keep in mind when shopping organic, that the produce may not appear pristine on the outside, but the flavor will outshine appearances and you may run into some pleasant surprises.

Get to know your farmer   Many of my friends are farmers and I feel blessed each time I receive a box of just-picked vegetables. I get to chat with them about their favorite crops, how they grew this year or perhaps some of their challenges. I know they appreciate the interest and loyalty in buying from them, over time. And remember, many farmers practice organic pesticide-free methods of farming, even if they can't afford to obtain official certification. Always ask to see if they are "organic".

Be creative   Go outside your comfort zone, explore and seek out the unusual, something you'd never find at your local supermarket.

Intelligent Packing   Remember to bring plenty of bags from home, even reusable produce bags, and don't forget to put the heavier items on the bottom of your basket or shopping bag. Beets, corn and potatoes go in first, with the softer veggies, lettuces, herbs and berries on top.

Beyond Produce   Many farmers markets feature local products, so don't overlook the other offerings from your community. Fresh local fish; breads and pastries; organic eggs and chicken; grass-fed beef, lamb and pork; locally made cheeses; nuts and oils, and, of course, flowers. Contribute to your local economy and support your local businesses.

TASTE
of SPAIN

No matter where you are in Spain, each meal begins with a basket full of fresh, crusty bread, fruity local olive oil and little bowls of glossy green and black table **olives**. Of course, it's impossible to write about Spanish food without talking about tapas. Tasty small plates, often given as a pre-dinner snack with drinks, offer the best from the sea and the garden and make for a perfectly elegant, relaxed evening.

The Spanish Mediterranean south coast and Santa Barbara share a very similar, temperate climate. Just like the Spanish, we are lucky to spend more time outside than we do indoors. Socializing in bars and restaurants is commonplace and, of course, as in Spain, food is an important part of our culture in Santa Barbara. I have a warm place in my heart for Spain, in particular the Andalucian region, where I lived for 5 years near Marbella and where my daughter was born. Oh, *"The Spain I Adore"*! I learned to live a different lifestyle, where the work day often does not start until 10 am and a mid-day siesta takes up a big part of the afternoon.

Many Sunday afternoons following a busy work week were spent at the sea at local **Chiringuitos**, the bar-restaurants right on the beach, similar to Greek tavernas. We saved our pesetas to indulge in grilled sardines, fresh off the boats, skewered and charred over hardwood fire, simply presented with lemon wedges, a huge plate of french fries and a large pitcher of **sangría**. The **Spaniards** have it right—a refreshing blend of flavors which makes for a flavorful and light cocktail are poured into the sangría, enjoyed with fresh fare. This is Mediterranean living.

AUTHENTIC SPANISH SANGRÍA

Perfect for any occasion, sangría can be made with a full-bodied red wine and slightly sweetened with loads of fruit. There are all sorts of twists on this classic Spanish recipe; honestly, you can use any type of fruit and wine. I love using the fruity, slightly spicy Spanish Tempranillo red. For a Sangría Blanco, I prefer a Spanish Albarino or Sauvignon Blanc—both of these wines can hold their own—with a dash of peach Schnapps or a splash of sparkling Cava. It is always best when left macerating to chill a few hours or overnight in the refrigerator.

4 TO 6 SERVINGS

1 apple or pear, washed and diced small

1 orange, washed and diced small

1 lemon, washed and diced small

1 oz Cointreau or Triple Sec

¼ cup brandy

1 (750 ml) bottle red wine – Spanish Tempranillo or any full-bodied red wine

6 oz sparkling lemonade (you can substitute sparkling water for a low-sugar version)

ice (optional on the side)

Chop the whole fruit into small pieces and place in a large glass pitcher. Add the Cointreau and brandy and mix well, to allow the fruit to release its natural juices. Add the wine and stir.

Add the sparkling lemonade or sparkling water and stir. (If you are making ahead of time, add the sparkling element just before your guests are about to arrive.)

Pour chilled sangría into glasses with lots of ice in a bowl on the side for guests to add if they want.

BUTTERNUT SQUASH EMPANADAS

Empanadas, baked or fried, are typically stuffed with meat, seafood or cheese.
You can put just about anything in a flaky little pastry, but seriously you have to try
these! Make the following recipe with homemade dough (see page 33)
or use your favorite store-bought puff pastry or pie dough in a pinch.

MAKES 12+

3 cups cooked butternut
  squash, cooled

1 teaspoon dried oregano

½ teaspoon crushed red
  chili flakes

½ teaspoon sea salt

¼ teaspoon freshly ground
  pepper

1 egg

1½ cups ricotta cheese

¼ cup grated Parmesan cheese

1 egg

1 tablespoon milk

sesame seeds to sprinkle

Place the cooked squash in a medium bowl and season
with oregano and red chili flakes, adding the salt and pepper
as well. (Cooked sweet potato works well too.)

In another bowl, lightly beat 1 egg and add the ricotta
and Parmesan cheeses, with a pinch of salt and pepper.
Cover and chill both fillings.

Preheat oven to 400°F and line a baking sheet pan with
parchment paper.

Roll the prepared dough out to ⅛-inch thin, using the homemade
dough, puff pastry or pie dough.

With a cookie cutter, cut the dough into 3-inch circles,
close enough together to form 12 circles.

Place 1 rounded spoonful of the chilled squash filling
and 1 spoonful of ricotta mixture onto the center of each circle.
Fold one half of the circle over the filling and form a half-moon
shape. Don't overfill your empanadas to allow easy folding.
Pinch the edges together with your fingers to seal the empanada
or you can also use the tines of a fork. Place each sealed
empanada onto the paper-lined baking pan.

In a small bowl, lightly beat the remaining egg with the milk
and brush the mixture over the empanadas. Sprinkle with sesame
seeds.

Bake at 400°F for 15 to 20 minutes, until the crust is golden.
Serve warm.

EMPANADA DOUGH

MAKES 12+

3 cups all-purpose flour

½ teaspoon sea salt

1 teaspoon sugar

½ cup plus 1 tablespoon unsalted butter, cold

½ cup vegetable shortening, cold

¾ cup ice water

In a large bowl, combine the flour, salt and sugar.

Cut the cold butter and shortening into ½-inch cubes. Sprinkle the cubes over the flour mixture and, with a pastry cutter or your fingers, work the flour mixture and butter until they are combined. Do not overmix—you should still be able to see small bits of butter.

Drizzle in the ice water and mix until the dough just comes together in a ball.

Pat the dough into a disk shape, wrap and refrigerate for at least one hour before rolling out.

ALBONDIGAS
SPANISH MEATBALLS

These meatballs are usually served in a small terra cotta dish, tapas style, smothered in a homemade tomato sauce, with plenty of bread on the side to sop it all up. They are perfect as an appetizer with some wine, but are also great as a main course with rice or pasta. With the Moroccan-influenced spices, they are addictive, so be sure to make plenty.

4 SERVINGS

1 lb ground meat, beef, pork, or a mix

2 cloves garlic, chopped

½ teaspoon ground cumin

½ teaspoon dried oregano

¼ teaspoon ground cinnamon

¼ teaspoon nutmeg

1 teaspoon sea salt and freshly ground pepper

1 large egg white, beaten

¼ cup olive oil, divided

FOR THE SAUCE

2 tablespoons olive oil

1 medium onion, finely chopped

1 teaspoon fennel seeds

1 teaspoon grated orange rind

½ teaspoon ground cumin

¼ teaspoon ground cinnamon

¼ teaspoon salt

¼ teaspoon cayenne pepper

1 28-oz can whole tomatoes, coarsely chopped

In a large mixing bowl, place the ground meats with the mixture of seasonings and the egg white and mix gently together until just combined. Dampen your hands slightly and form the meat mixture into meatballs, about 1 inch in diameter.

In a heavy-bottomed frying pan, heat up about 2 tablespoons olive oil and cook the meatballs in batches over medium-high heat, until browned on all sides. Remove the cooked meatballs to a paper-towel-lined plate and set aside.

For the sauce, wipe out the frying pan that you used for the meatballs, return it to medium heat and add the remaining 2 tablespoons olive oil. Add the chopped onion and cook until golden brown, about 5 minutes. Stir in all the seasonings and the chopped tomatoes and allow to simmer for about 10 minutes. Add the meatballs, cover, and let cook together for about 5 minutes longer to reheat. Serve 3-4 meatballs with the sauce in a small terra cotta dish for individual portions or in a large casserole for the table.

GAZPACHO ANDALUZ

Having lived in the Andalusia region in Malaga, Spain, I often make this drink-appetizer.
Every region in Spain has its own variety, the most popular being the *Gazpacho Andaluz*,
where it originates from. To serve as a starter, rim the glasses with coarse sea salt
just before serving and make this in the morning so it's well chilled.
A great way to use your over-ripe homegrown tomatoes and other bounties
from your summer garden.

MAKES 1 QUART

- 2 slices country bread, broken into big chunks
- 2 lbs very ripe tomatoes, coarsely chopped
- 1 cucumber, peeled, seeded, and coarsely chopped
- ½ small white onion, coarsely chopped
- 1 red bell pepper, seeds and pith removed, coarsely chopped
- 2 garlic cloves, peeled
- 1 teaspoon sea salt
- ½ teaspoon Spanish *pimentón* (smoked paprika)
- 2 tablespoons Spanish sherry vinegar (or apple cider vinegar)
- ½ cup cold water
- ½ cup good quality olive oil

Put bread chunks in a medium bowl with chopped tomatoes, cucumber, red pepper, onion, garlic, salt and ¼ cup olive oil. Mix to combine and let sit for 30 minutes to macerate the flavors; the salt pulls some moisture out of the tomatoes. (This certainly can be made without the bread if you prefer.)

Puree the tomato-bread mixture in a high speed blender with the smoked *pimentón*, sherry vinegar, and remaining ¼ cup olive oil. Blend in the cold water to loosen the mixture and make it a "drinkable" consistency, as generally it is served in small glasses. Taste and add more salt as needed. Transfer to a large pitcher and chill for at least 2 hours before serving.

SALPICÓN DE MARISCOS
SPANISH SEAFOOD SALAD

One of many versions of this dish is found in almost every tapas bar in Spain. This very simple salad can be prepared in minutes and it's absolutely delicious. Make in advance and serve cold, dressed with the smoked paprika vinaigrette.

4 SERVINGS

3 cups cooked mixed seafood - shrimp, lobster, octopus, mussels, or squid, cut into small pieces

½ cup ripe tomatoes, chopped

½ cup mixed pitted olives, chopped

½ cup red onion, chopped

1 roasted red pepper, chopped

3 sprigs fresh mint, chopped

3 sprigs fresh parsley, chopped

FOR SMOKED PAPRIKA VINAIGRETTE

1 cup good quality olive oil, such as Spanish Arbequina

¼ cup sherry vinegar

1 tablespoon Dijon mustard

1 tablespoon smoked paprika, Pimentón de la Vera

2 garlic cloves, peeled

sea salt and freshly ground pepper, to taste

In a medium bowl combine a mix of seafood with the chopped tomatoes, olives, onion, roasted pepper and chopped fresh herbs.

In a blender, combine all the dressing ingredients and purée until smooth.

Stir the seafood together with some of the vinaigrette and chill, covered, until serving.

Store any remaining vinaigrette in a glass jar in the refrigerator for up to 2 weeks.

TORTILLITAS DE CAMARONES
SHRIMP FRITTERS

These are wonderful little nibbles! Great on their own, or serve them with the same Smoky Tomato-Garlic Alioli featured in the Patatas Bravas recipe on page 45. It definitely adds another layer of flavor.

MAKES 20 SMALL FRITTERS

1 large onion, peeled and quartered

1 fennel bulb, peeled and quartered

1 garlic clove, minced

2 cups raw shrimp, peeled and deveined

2 large organic eggs

½ cup brown rice flour

½ cup all-purpose flour (or gluten-free garbanzo bean flour)

¼ teaspoon baking soda

¼ teaspoon smoked paprika

⅛ teaspoon cayenne pepper

½ teaspoon freshly ground pepper

2 teaspoons sea salt mixed with ½ teaspoon ground fennel seed

olive oil for cooking

Add the onion, fennel and garlic in the bowl of a food processor and pulse until minced. Add the peeled shrimp and continue to pulse until minced, then add 2 eggs to combine.

Remove this mixture to a medium bowl and add in the rice and all-purpose flours, baking soda, paprika, peppers, and 1 teaspoon salt; mix until just combined. (Avoid overmixing, which can make the mixture starchy and gooey.)

Heat the skillet on medium heat for 2 minutes and add just enough olive oil to coat the bottom of the pan.

In batches, drop spoonfuls of the mixture into the hot oil without crowding. Fry about 2 to 3 minutes until each side has a golden brown crust. With a spatula, transfer the fritters to a paper towel to soak up the excess oil. Sprinkle immediately with some of the fennel sea salt to serve.

N O T E You want to hear the sizzle, make sure the pan has been preheated, so the fritters get a golden brown crust. Determine the size of your pan by whether you want mini bites for appetizers or a larger small-plate first course.

ALMEJAS À LA GADITANA
CLAMS IN SHERRY SAUCE

Another version of tapas, this one highlighting Santa Barbara's shellfish.
This classic Andalusian seafood dish is traditionally served with lots of crusty bread
to soak up the peppery broth, rich with Spanish sherry from the Jerez region
in the province of Cádiz. Serve chilled Fino as an aperitif wine, along with this dish.
Once all the ingredients are prepped, it's ready to eat in 10 minutes.

4 SERVINGS

3 tablespoons olive oil

5 cloves garlic, finely chopped

2 tablespoons diced chorizo

3 lbs (about 3 dozen) small
clams (littlenecks),
scrubbed clean

1 cup dry white wine

½ cup Fino Jerez sherry
or California sherry

¼ cup finely chopped parsley

2 small red Thai chiles,
stemmed and finely
chopped

sea salt and freshly ground
pepper, to taste

country bread, sliced and
toasted, for serving

Heat olive oil in a medium saucepan over medium-high heat.
Add garlic and chorizo and cook quickly, stirring until fragrant,
about 1 minute. Add the clams, wine, sherry, parsley, and chiles;
season with salt and pepper. Bring to a boil, and cook, covered,
until the clams open, about 10 minutes. Uncover the pan
and remove and discard any clams that didn't open. Pour into
a large serving bowl with all the broth. Serve with warm bread
on the side.

PATATAS BRAVAS
OVEN ROASTED POTATOES

Native to Spain, Patatas Bravas are to Spanish tapas bars what chicken wings are to American sports bars. These crisp potatoes, covered in a creamy, slightly smoky mayonnaise-based sauce, are a great late-night bar snack.

6 SERVINGS

3 lbs small potatoes, fingerlings or Yukon Gold, quartered lengthwise

2 tablespoons olive oil

coarse sea salt and freshly ground pepper

minced parsley, for garnish (optional)

FOR SMOKY TOMATO-GARLIC ALIOLI

½ small yellow onion, thinly sliced

3 cloves fresh garlic, peeled and sliced

1 teaspoon olive oil

1 teaspoon smoked Spanish paprika

¼ teaspoon sugar

2 tablespoons sun-dried tomatoes, drained

splash of sherry vinegar

pinch of cayenne pepper

sea salt and freshly ground pepper, to taste

½ cup good quality mayonnaise

½ cup fat free Greek yogurt

Preheat oven to 400°F. Line a baking sheet with parchment paper.

Soak the cut potatoes in cold water for 30 minutes. Drain and pat dry. Toss with 2 tablespoons olive oil and ½ teaspoon each salt and pepper. Spread evenly on the parchment-lined baking sheet and bake 35-40 minutes, tossing once halfway through, until browned.

While the potatoes are roasting in the oven, make the alioli. First, sauté the sliced onion and garlic in a small skillet with the olive oil, for just a minute or so.

In a food processor or blender, pulse the sautéed onion and garlic with the smoked paprika, sugar, sun-dried tomatoes, sherry vinegar, cayenne and salt and pepper until coarsely ground. Add the mayonnaise and yogurt to combine and set aside in the refrigerator. Makes about 1½ cups.

Once potatoes are crispy, transfer to a serving platter, season with coarse salt and drizzle with the smoky tomato-garlic alioli. Garnish with fresh parsley and serve hot.

ROMESCO SAUCE

Romesco sauce has its roots in the Spanish province of Catalonia.
Although the mixture has lots of variations, most combine roasted red peppers, nuts,
garlic, and crusty bread to make a thick sauce that often accompanies grilled fish
and meats. Top your favorite chicken recipe with the sauce or bake in this sauce
for a savory option.

MAKES 3 CUPS

2 cups tomatoes cut into quarters (about 5 large Roma tomatoes)

1 cup roasted red peppers (use jarred or roast your own for a smokier flavor)

½ cup olive oil

1 tablespoon Spanish sherry vinegar or apple cider vinegar

2 tablespoons garlic, peeled and sliced

1 tablespoon Spanish smoked paprika

2 tablespoons balsamic vinegar

½ teaspoon red chili flakes

1 teaspoon sea salt (or to taste)

This recipe uses Roma tomatoes, but canned tomatoes can be used when ripe fresh tomatoes are not in season. Commonly using almonds and bread, I have developed this nut and gluten-free version. It is equally good on roasted potatoes, white beans with arugula or stir a few spoonfuls into scrambled eggs. For a mouth-watering appetizer, slice a goat cheese log into 1-inch medallions into an ovenproof dish, spoon romesco sauce on top, and broil until the cheese is melty. Serve with bread or crackers.

Place the ingredients as listed in a blender or food processor and puree for 1 minute. Store in a glass jar in the fridge for up to 1 week.

ROSEMARY-ALMOND OLIVE OIL CAKE

Olive oil enhances the flavor and maintains the moist texture
of this Mediterranean-inspired cake. Casual yet elegant, it's a fine conclusion
for a dinner party or to use as a birthday cake.

12 SERVINGS

1 cup whole wheat flour

1 cup all-purpose flour
  (or gluten-free flour blend)

½ cup ground almond meal

½ cup fine cornmeal

¾ cup sugar

½ teaspoon sea salt

½ teaspoon baking soda

1 teaspoon baking powder

2 teaspoons vanilla extract

1 teaspoon almond extract

2 teaspoons fresh rosemary,
  finely chopped

½ cup good quality olive oil

2 cups sweetened almond
  milk or other milk
  substitute

2 eggs

1 tablespoon orange blossom
  water

1 tablespoon freshly grated
  orange zest

1 tablespoon apple cider
  vinegar

FOR ORANGE SYRUP

½ cup agave mixed with
  1 tablespoon orange
  flower water

Preheat oven to 350°F. Butter and flour a 9-inch round cake pan
for 12 pieces of cake.

Double the recipe and bake several rounds to stack for a birthday
cake or use the double batch in a 13x9 inch rectangular cake pan
for 24 pieces of cake.

Measure and stir together all the dry ingredients in a medium
bowl.

Measure and whisk together all the wet ingredients in a large
mixing bowl and fold the dry ingredients into the wet until just
combined.

Pour batter into the cake tin. Bake in the center of the oven
for 35-45 minutes until a toothpick inserted in center comes
out dry. Cool in the pan for 15 minutes on a wire rack, then
remove from the pan onto a wire rack and brush with the orange
blossom-scented agave syrup, cooling completely. Decorate the
top with a sugar glaze or your favorite frosting or filling, or
simply sprinkle with powdered sugar. Serve with fresh sliced
oranges and sliced almonds.

CHOCOLATE PISTACHIO BRITTLE BARK

I am more addicted to chocolate than I am to any other dessert. A small piece of this super-chunky dark-chocolate bark brings a big smile to my face. As we were all happy to learn, researchers have found that eating chocolate—the number one food craved by women— causes the brain to release endorphins, those chemicals that make us feel good. Make a double batch and be sure to hide your own stash in a secret spot.

1 lb good quality dark chocolate (60 to 70 percent)

1 cup roasted shelled pistachios

¾ cup dried fruits (mixed cranberries, currants, chopped figs)

coarse sea salt to sprinkle on top

Line a baking sheet with parchment paper. Using a sharp knife, finely chop the chocolate.

In a bowl set over a saucepan of gently simmering water, heat the chopped chocolate, stirring occasionally, until it is about two-thirds melted; be careful not let the bowl touch the water. Remove the bowl from the saucepan and stir the chocolate until it is completely melted and the temperature registers 90°F on a candy thermometer. If the chocolate has not melted completely and is still too cool, set it over the saucepan for 1 or 2 minutes longer, stirring constantly; do not overheat.

Stir the pistachios and dried fruits into the chocolate and spread onto the prepared baking sheet in a ½-inch thick layer, making sure the nuts and seeds are completely covered in chocolate. Refrigerate the bark for about 5 minutes, sprinkle on some sea salt, then continue to refrigerate until hardened. Invert the bark onto a work surface. Remove the parchment paper, break into pieces and store (run and hide this) until ready to serve.

TASTE
of PROVENCE

I literally spent 'A Day in Provence' when first visiting Nice back in 1992. After an impromptu change of travel plans, I picked up my longtime friend, cookbook author Pamela Sheldon Johns at the Milan airport. Pamela flew in to "save me". We drove a rented Renault down to Nice that afternoon, switchback turns, back and forth down the winding road to the **Cote d'Azur**. She most certainly recalls our trip with more detail. I remember waiting for the guy on the bicycle to arrive with the classic chickpea flatbread, **Socca**—the Niçoise street food served in the heart of the Old Town at the famed Cours Saleya Market—eating it right away while it was still steaming hot from a paper cone. "The atmosphere here is very friendly and the scents of fresh produce, from **olive oil** to sun-ripened tomatoes and **aromatic herbs** to lovely flowers, seem to put everyone in a good mood." What I took away from this trip was the exceptionally crafted Alziari olive oil, made using ancestral techniques in a historic mill, and bags of aromatic **herbes de Provence**, crafted from local herbs common to this region containing a blend of savory, marjoram, rosemary, thyme, oregano, and **lavender**.

The sun shines nearly year-round and stunning seaside locations dot this **Mediterranean** coastline. As we ate our way along the coast, we stopped on the way in Monaco, choosing the simplest of fare to snack on. We feasted on local cheeses, olives and fresh breads, while making our way through to the Cinque Terre. Provençal cuisine is savored with uncomplicated recipes with a flair devoted to the bountiful local ingredients we often see here in Santa Barbara.

Provence

PROVENCE LAVENDER APERITIF

This refreshing cocktail featuring gin, Cointreau and vermouth mixed with a botanical lavender syrup and fresh oranges is uniquely aromatic thanks to its herbal, lavender and citrus notes, reminiscent of sunny Provence in the south of France.

MAKES 2 COCKTAILS

1 orange, sliced thin, for muddling

3 oz gin

2 oz dry vermouth

1 oz Cointreau liqueur

2 tablespoons Provence lavender syrup

ice, to serve

2 sprigs of fresh lavender, for garnish

Muddle a few orange slices in a cocktail shaker.

Add the rest of the ingredients (except garnish) and stir.

Strain into tall chilled glasses and garnish with a sprig of fresh lavender.

LAVENDER SYRUP

A subtle blend of lavender flowers and herbes de Provence makes for a pleasant, refreshing cordial perfect for a summer's day! Stir the syrup into lemonade, teas, champagne or cocktails. Drizzle on pound cake, waffles and fruit or whisk a few spoonfuls into whipped cream. Make this in early summer, when the lavender flowers are still fresh!

MAKES ABOUT 1½ CUPS SYRUP

½ cup granulated organic sugar

1 ½ cups water

½ cup fresh organic edible lavender flowers (or 2 tablespoons dried lavender flowers)

2 teaspoons herbes de Provence (optional)

1 small fresh lemon, juiced

Heat sugar and water in a saucepan over medium heat; stir to dissolve the sugar completely.

Bring to a boil and remove from heat. Add the lavender flowers (and the herbes de Provence, if using). Cover and let the flowers steep for 1 hour.

Pour through a fine mesh strainer or paper coffee filter into a measuring glass (with a lip for easy pouring). Stir in fresh lemon juice.

Pour into a clean bottle (preferably sterilized), cap, and refrigerate for up to 2 weeks, or freeze for up to 6 weeks.

PISSALADIERE

Originating from Nice in southern France, pissalidiere is a classic with its thin, pizza-like crust piled with caramelized onions, anchovies, olives, and fresh herbs. Pissaladiere is often made with puff pastry, but a good pizza dough can always be substituted. As anchovies are NOT appreciated by everyone, in my experience, there doesn't seem to be an in-between, so use optionally.

4 SERVINGS

one sheet puff pastry
  or pizza dough

1 6-oz can anchovies, packed
  in olive oil (optional)

12-15 oil-cured black olives,
  pitted and roughly
  chopped

1 cup caramelized onions,
  see recipe below

½ teaspoon fresh thyme
  leaves

FOR CARAMELIZED ONIONS

¼ cup extra virgin olive oil

3 lbs onions, peeled
  and thinly sliced

sea salt and freshly ground
  pepper

Preheat oven to 375°F.

Line a baking pan with parchment paper. If using puff pastry dough, cut into a long rectangle; if using pizza dough, place your rolled out pizza dough on parchment paper into desired shape.

Remove the anchovies from the can and break into small pieces. Reserve the anchovy oil. Press the anchovy pieces into the dough and measure out 2-3 teaspoons of the reserved anchovy oil. Smear the oil over the entire surface. Press the olives into the dough and finish with the caramelized onions on top.

Bake at 375°F for 35-40 minutes or until the crust is golden brown. Remove from the oven and sprinkle with fresh thyme leaves. Slice into wedges and serve warm or at room temperature.

For the caramelized onions, heat oil in a large saute pan over medium-low heat. Add onions and season generously with salt and pepper. Cover the pan to let the onions slowly simmer for 30 minutes, stirring occasionally. Uncover and continue cooking until the moisture has evaporated and the onions cook down to a very tender marmalade-like consistency, 20-30 minutes. Remove from heat and set aside.

SOCCA

My first time eating socca was with my good friend, the award-winning cookbook author Pamela Sheldon Johns, when we took a side trip to the southern coast of France and spent a day in Nice nearly 25 years ago. I recall watching the street vendor meticulously create these crisp crepes, cooking in a huge pan on a stove in the daily market. The result was this peppery chickpea crepe.
This simple batter, with nothing more than chickpea flour, water, and olive oil, happens to be gluten free and can be used as a gluten–free crust with toppings.

MAKES TWO 9-INCH CREPES

1 cup garbanzo bean flour, sifted

1¼ cups water

1 tablespoon olive oil, plus more for cooking

½ teaspoon sea salt

½ teaspoon freshly ground pepper

In a bowl, whisk all ingredients together, then let the mixture rest for at least 30 minutes, allowing the flour to absorb the liquid.

Preheat oven to 400°F and place a medium cast-iron skillet in the oven for 10 minutes. Using oven mitts, remove the skillet and coat with a generous amount of olive oil; this will be soaked up into the crepe.

Position the oven rack on the upper level. Pour about half of the batter in the skillet, swirling it around to spread the batter out, and place the skillet on the oven rack; bake for about 10 minutes. The edges will start to get crispy and the batter should be firm in the center, not runny. The top will be slightly browned. Flip the socca out of the pan onto a serving plate.

Repeat for the second crepe, adding more olive oil to the hot pan. If you prefer a slightly crispier crepe, place the finished crepes on a baking sheet and return to the oven for a few minutes. Simply eat as is or layer with toppings.

CELERY ROOT-LEEK SOUP

Celery root or celeriac tastes a bit like a cross between celery and a potato and cooks much faster than other root vegetables. I was craving a creamy potato-leek soup when I came up short on potatoes but had two large celery roots on hand. This soup is now my favorite—love these unplanned mishaps. Prepare with a bone broth or vegetable broth (both work well here) with caramelized diced apple to garnish and a generous drizzle of olive oil.

4 SERVINGS

3 tablespoons butter

2 leeks, ends removed and sliced thinly, washed very well

3 cloves garlic, minced

1-inch piece ginger, minced

4 cups bone or vegetable broth

2 pounds celeriac, peeled and cut into 1½-inch chunks

1 tablespoon apple cider vinegar

½ teaspoon sea salt

1 apple, diced and sauteed in olive oil

4 tablespoons good quality olive oil

Heat a heavy-bottomed pot on medium heat, add butter and the leeks and cook for a few minutes, stirring. Add the garlic and ginger and cook for another couple of minutes. Add the broth, celeriac, apple cider vinegar and salt and bring to a boil. Turn down to a simmer, cover, and cook for 15 minutes, or until celeriac is soft.

Transfer to a blender and process until well pureed, adding more broth if needed.

Season to taste with salt as needed. Divide into 4 serving bowls, scatter the sauteed apples on top and drizzle with olive oil.

TAPENADE

I didn't know until recently that its name comes from the Provençal word for capers, *tapenas*. Consisting of puréed or finely chopped olives, capers, anchovies and olive oil, it is a popular food in the south of France, where it is generally eaten as an hors d'œuvre. It takes less than 5 minutes to make and is eaten simply with a slice of grilled bread or served as a condiment on fish or a sandwich spread.

MAKES 1 CUP

½ cup pitted black olives (use a flavorful variety)

¼ cup good quality olive oil

1 tablespoon fresh lemon juice

½ teaspoon fresh lemon zest

1 tablespoon capers, drained

2 garlic cloves, peeled

3 anchovy fillets, canned, oil-packed

1 teaspoon fresh thyme, or ½ teaspoon dried thyme

freshly ground pepper

baguette slices or vegetables for serving

Place the olives, olive oil, lemon juice, zest, drained capers, garlic, anchovies, thyme, and black pepper in a food processor. Process by pulsing until all the ingredients are finely chopped, but not completely pureed. Serve the olive spread on baguette slices or with fresh crudités.

AIOLI

Aioli sounds fancy, but it's really just a garlicky mayonnaise. I use a combination of vegetable and olive oils since an aioli of solely extra virgin olive oil can be overpowering and expensive. You can just as easily swap the grapeseed oil for more olive oil if you prefer the more assertive flavor.

MAKES 1 CUP

2 medium garlic cloves

1 teaspoon Dijon mustard

1 large egg

fresh saffron, generous pinch of threads

½ cup extra virgin olive oil

½ cup grapeseed or vegetable oil

2 teaspoons freshly squeezed lemon juice

sea salt

Place the garlic, mustard, egg and saffron in the bowl of a food processor fitted with a blade attachment. Process until evenly combined, about 10 seconds.

With the motor running, slowly add olive oil in a thin stream, followed by the grapeseed oil, until completely combined, about 2 minutes. Stop the processor, add the lemon juice, season with salt, and pulse until thoroughly mixed. Stop and scrape down the sides of the bowl with a rubber spatula, then pulse until all ingredients are evenly incorporated. Let sit for at least 30 minutes before using, to allow the flavors to meld together. Refrigerate in a container with a tight-fitting lid for up to 3 days.

ANCHOÏADE

When I was in Provence, our host, Claudine, served a delicious anchoïade for lunch the first day, with a bowl of assorted crudités bought fresh from the market that morning. Claudine's anchoïade had the consistency of a thin mayonnaise. A Provençal puree of anchovies, garlic, olive oil and vinegar, often slathered on grilled bread or served as a dip, is essentially an aioli with the addition of anchovies. Anchoïade, pronounced ah~/shoh/yahd, can accompany boiled eggs, fish, or steamed vegetables like potatoes, carrots, green beans and cauliflower.

MAKES 1 CUP

1 7-oz can anchovies, packed in oil, drained

2 cloves garlic, peeled and thinly sliced

1 tablespoon red wine vinegar

½ cup good quality olive oil

Combine the anchovies and garlic in a mortar and grind them into a thick paste (alternatively, use a food processor).

Transfer to a bowl, add the vinegar, then whisk in the olive oil, a little at a time, until the mixture gets to the desired consistency—thin, if using as a sauce, or thick, if serving as a dip.

NOTE Blanched *green beans* are easy to dip; long beans also come in purple, white, and yellow at some markets and add extra color on your crudité platter. Consider crunchy *jicama* as a sweeter alternative to celery. Peel, then cut into strips or half-moon shape and top with a squeeze of lemon. A summer farmers market staple, young *kohlrabi* can be eaten raw and tastes faintly like broccoli stems. Pare away the thicker outer skin, then cut into matchsticks or very thin rounds. The crisp anise flavor of *fennel* cuts through creamy dips, and pairs exceptionally well with aioli or tapenade.

Slice peppery radishes in half the long way. If you can find them at your farmers market, *carrots* come in various colors like purple, gold, or pale yellow. To keep as much of the color as possible, scrub carrots to remove all soil and don't peel them.

Thin *asparagus* might not need to be cooked. *Sugar snap peas*, in their edible pods, are perfect for bite-size dipping and eating, and you can serve them raw as well.

Make sure to remove any stems and strings beforehand; use a paring knife to make it go faster. Serve with your favorite spread or dip.

THREE BEAN SALAD WITH TUNA

I have a weakness for beans, and mixed with oil-cured tuna, this is the most amazing salad I've ever tasted. There are so many beans available, you can experiment with different types. I used fresh French beans (*haricot verts*), flageolet and garbanzo beans, mixed with oil-cured tuna, green olives, shaved fennel, onion and radish. When using dry beans, you may have to plan ahead; canned beans may be the closest thing to creating your own addiction.

4 SERVINGS

1 cup French beans
   (*haricot verts*)

1 14-oz can garbanzo beans,
   drained and rinsed

½ cup flageolet beans, cooked

1 fennel bulb, washed and
   finely sliced

1 small red onion, finely sliced

2-3 radishes, washed
   and finely sliced

2 tablespoons green olives,
   roughly chopped

2 tablespoons extra virgin
   olive oil

1 tablespoon wine vinegar

1 tablespoon Dijon mustard

½ lemon, zest and juice

sea salt and freshly ground
   pepper

1 6-oz can Albacore tuna,
   packed in oil, drained
   and flaked

Bring a large saucepan of water to a boil and cook the green beans for 3 minutes; drain and refresh in ice cold water. In a large salad bowl, mix the other beans, fennel, red onion, radishes and olives and add the cooled green beans.

In a glass bottle or bowl, mix the olive oil, vinegar, mustard and lemon juice. Season with salt and pepper and toss through the salad until well coated. Add the tuna; be careful not to break up the pieces too much.

The tossed salad will keep for a day in the refrigerator. You can also prepare everything in advance, keeping the dressing separate and tossing with the other ingredients just before serving so beans keep their bright green color.

SALMON NIÇOISE

Preparations for this salad are simple, allowing the fresh flavors to shine through. This is a twist on the French classic using seared salmon instead of tuna, and adorned with slender asparagus, tomatoes, eggs and new potatoes, adding other summer ripe garden veggies like fennel, artichokes or mild spring onions.

4 SERVINGS

2 8-oz salmon fillet,
   with skin, deboned

sea salt and freshly ground
   pepper

2 tablespoons olive oil

8 new potatoes, halved

1 lb asparagus, trimmed

3 large free range eggs

1 head butter lettuce

1 handful black olives

4 ripe plum tomatoes

Season salmon fillets with salt and pepper and add skin-side down, to a hot frying pan with 2 tablespoons of olive oil. Fry for 4 minutes on medium high heat, then turn and cook for another 2 minutes. Remove from the pan and set aside to cool. The cooled salmon can be left whole or flaked into chunks.

In a medium pot of boiling salted water, boil the asparagus until tender, about 5 minutes. Remove with a slotted spoon and refresh in ice-cold water.

Cook the new potatoes in the same boiling water until just tender, about 12 minutes. Strain and allow to cool. Do not rinse the potatoes in water.

Cook the eggs in a small pan of boiling water for 8 minutes until hard boiled. Remove, rinse under cool water, peel and quarter.

While the eggs are cooking, tear the lettuce into pieces, and cut the tomatoes into wedges.

Compose all the cooked ingredients on a serving platter and drizzle with a homemade dressing, olive-caper vinaigrette or arugula vinaigrette.

OLIVE-CAPER VINAIGRETTE

A versatile dressing which has the essence of Provencal flavors and adds
a punch of flavor drizzled on roasted chicken breast, Salmon Niçoise Salad
or served along with crusty bread.

MAKES ABOUT 1 CUP

4 tablespoons extra virgin
  olive oil

¼ cup lemon juice, fresh

1 teaspoon Dijon mustard

2 tablespoons capers, drained

2 tablespoons black olives,
  minced

1 clove of garlic, peeled,
  finely chopped

½ teaspoon finely ground
  lavender

sea salt and freshly ground
  pepper

In a medium bowl whisk together the extra virgin olive oil,
lemon juice, Dijon mustard, capers and minced olives
with a pinch of sea salt and pepper. Add finely chopped garlic
and ground lavender to combine.

CHERRY CLAFOUTI

This classic French recipe calls for basic ingredients: butter, eggs, milk, flour, salt, sugar, vanilla and, of course, cherries. In France, clafouti is made with the pits, but I find that pitting the cherries first makes this treat more appetizing and easier to eat. Any fresh berry will work in place of cherries; using golden raspberries or blackberries is a good option. Typically served as dessert, the leftovers can be savored for breakfast or brunch as well.

6-8 SERVINGS

2 cups fresh sweet cherries, stemmed, washed and pitted

2 tablespoons butter, melted, plus 2 teaspoons for baking dish

½ cup sugar, plus 2 teaspoons for baking dish

4 eggs

¼ teaspoon salt

¾ cup flour

1 cup milk

½ teaspoon almond extract

½ teaspoon vanilla extract

¼ cup powdered sugar, for dusting

Preheat the oven to 350°F. Butter a round 10-inch quiche pan or baking dish. Dust with about 2 tablespoons of sugar. Arrange the cherries in the dish in a single layer; set aside until you prepare the batter, which is similar to a crepe mixture, and can easily be prepared in a blender.

If mixing by hand, whisk the eggs with ½ cup of sugar and the salt, in a medium bowl. Stir in flour, milk, and vanilla and almond extracts and mix until well blended. Add 2 tablespoons melted butter and stir to combine. Pour the mixture over the cherries in the dish.

Bake for about 40-45 minutes until puffed and golden brown. Cool on a rack for a few minutes while it deflates. Sprinkle with powdered sugar before serving. Serve warm or chilled.

TASTE
of ITALIA

Highlights of some of my favorite foods and liquid refreshments with a Tuscan flair, in season both here and in Italia. For a refreshing drink, sip on a **Sgroppino**—a pre-dinner blend of lemon sorbet, vodka, and Prosecco. It's like a grownup version of a summertime lemon slushy. In Italy, April is the month of artichoke festivals. Artichokes grow in abundance in and around the Santa Barbara area as well and they are both a challenge and a joy to prepare.

On my last visit to Tuscany, every trattoria, osteria and *ristorante* had artichokes on their menu. The most celebrated preparation of the *carciofo romanesco* in Tuscany is "*alla giudia*". This Jewish-style artichoke is deep fried whole, until golden brown, making the leaves crispy and light. My **Crispy Artichoke Chips** make a great crunchy snack. This quick version is satisfying on its own, with a cocktail or used as a garnish.

Italia.

Tuscan people worship their bread, their olive oil and the traditional **bruschetta**, which in Florence is known as *fettunta*. Make this to begin your meal—a toasted or grilled slice of Tuscan bread rubbed with fresh garlic, generously drizzled with a fragrant local olive oil and sparingly sprinkled with salt. A few spoonfuls of **olive tapenade** will add just that perfect amount of saltiness to the bruschetta. Use this crunchy bread to finish off a typical **Panzanella** salad, filled with the summer's best ripe tomatoes, cucumbers and onions, and sprinkled with capers.

Tuscan White Beans with Shrimp tossed in my mild **Arugula Vinaigrette** served with a side of Artichokes, Fresh Peas and Fava Beans round out this meal.

After a feast like this, what could be better than *Cantuccini*, almond biscotti that are made from scratch in Tuscany. Do as the Italians do and serve them with a glass of the very potent **Vin Santo**, a very nice digestive liqueur. *Cantuccini* are great for dunking in coffee or tea, as well as for an afternoon pick-me-up.

SGROPPINO AL LIMONE COCKTAIL

This slushy combination of lemon sorbet, vodka, and Prosecco is common in Italy as a refreshing palate cleanser or a pre-dinner drink. Limoncello, the Italian lemon liqueur, is added for a punch of lemon flavor.

MAKES 4 DRINKS

2 cups (16 oz) good quality lemon sorbet, softened

2 tablespoons Limoncello, optional

4 tablespoons vodka

1 cup sparkling wine or Italian Prosecco wine, chilled

zest of one lemon

Chill four champagne flutes, tall glasses, or goblets.

In a medium bowl, gently whisk Limoncello, vodka and Prosecco into the lemon sorbet until smooth.

Do not use a blender or whisk too much or it will become too liquid. Pour mixture into the chilled champagne flutes. Sprinkle lemon zest on top.

NOTE The drinks will separate if left standing, so do this just before serving

CRISPY ARTICHOKE CHIPS

I made this stellar snack quite by accident when testing out a recipe for a vegan
client, wanting a crisp substitute for bacon. I painstakingly dried
and fried eggplants, beets and potatoes, obvious replacements, and found
artichokes to be just that perfect consistency. You can enjoy them simply on their
own for an appetizer with a cocktail or use as a garnish.
Even though fried, these artichoke chips are very light and big on flavor;
add a sprinkling of infused salt and fresh herbs.

4 SERVINGS

8-10 baby artichokes
2 cups brown rice flour
2 quarts vegetable oil
sea salt to taste
fresh herbs and lemon
    for garnish

Bring vegetable oil slowly to 350°F in a large skillet, using
a thermometer to test the temperature.

Peel the tough outer skins off the baby artichokes and remove
the thistles on top.

Shave the artichokes as thinly as possible, or simply peel
the tender leaves off one by one.

Toss the slices in brown rice flour, lightly coating them.

Deep fry in the hot oil until they turn brown and crispy, careful
not to burn them.

Remove with a strainer or slotted spoon onto a paper towel
to remove the excess oil.

Sprinkle generously with fennel infused salt, or your favorite sea
salt to taste.

NOTE Sliced mushrooms can be fried the same way.

CROSTINI DI PROSCIUTTO

Another simple appetizer created by chance—after baking slices of prosciutto
to top a Caesar salad, I thought, how can I make these into crispy cups.
Easily enough it turns out, by placing thin slices of prosciutto into mini muffin
tins and baking them until crunchy, then filling them with a mixture
of white beans, red pepper, tomato, and basil. These can be made ahead of time
and assembled just before serving. Use your imagination for other fillings,
such as mozzarella, basil and tomato, a peppery goat cheese spread,
or even scrambled eggs.

MAKES ABOUT 24 MINI CUPS

**6-oz package of prosciutto
(about 12 slices)**

¼ cup cooked white beans

**1 roasted bell pepper,
finely diced**

2 Roma tomatoes, finely diced

1 teaspoon minced basil

olive oil

**sea salt and freshly ground
pepper**

fresh chives for garnish

Preheat oven to 375°F. Slice prosciutto down the middle to make
2 long thinner strips.

Lay each half slice inside a mini muffin tin. Overlap the sides
to make a "meat cup."

Bake for 10-12 minutes. Remove from the oven and allow to cool
for a couple minutes. Place on a paper towel to drain off
any excess fat. The prosciutto "cups" will firm up once cool.

In a small bowl, combine the ingredients for the filling
with a dash of olive oil to hold them together, season with salt
and pepper to taste and spoon into each cup.

NOTE You can use right away, or refrigerate the cups
and the filling separately until ready to use. Bring to room
temperature before using and crisp for just a few moments
in a hot oven before filling, if needed.

FETTUNTA

In Italy, this simple *fettunta*—or "greased slice"—is made to celebrate the first olive oil of the season. It's simply grilled bread, rubbed with a fresh clove of garlic, drizzled with the best olive oil you have, and then sprinkled with coarse sea salt. How great is that ?! Excellent on its own with just the garlic, you can also add a topping to make bruschetta, or add it torn up to a panzanella salad. I love it with sliced tomatoes as a breakfast favorite or topped with avocado for a quick, satisfying lunch.

4 SERVINGS

1 small loaf good quality bread,
   1-inch thick slices

4 whole fresh garlic cloves,
   peeled

good quality olive oil

sea salt

Toast or grill slices of bread until crisp. Swipe the fresh garlic clove over the entire surface of the toasted bread slice a few times. Drizzle with olive oil and sprinkle with sea salt.

PANZANELLA

It is a mortal sin to throw stale bread away. Tuscan farmers use their bread leftovers to make a summer bread salad. I love this part of summer, with all the fresh tomatoes and basil. This great summer salad uses all those sun-ripened vegetables, seasoned heartily with olive oil and vinegar. My favorite way to prepare the bread for this is using the fettunta method. Other variations call for oil-cured tuna or fresh mozzarella bocconcini, added to the basic salad recipe.

4 SERVINGS

1 small loaf good quality bread

2 whole large garlic cloves, peeled

2 cups cherry tomatoes, sliced in half

1 cup cucumber, diced

2 tablespoons capers, drained

1 small bunch basil leaves

3 tablespoons good quality olive oil

2 tablespoons wine vinegar

sea salt and freshly ground pepper

If you can't grill outside, heat a grill pan on the stove. Slice the bread into 1-inch slices.

Grill both sides until golden. Rub the grilled bread with the raw garlic clove, swiping it across the entire surface. Tear the bread into bite-size chunks and place in a large serving bowl. Add the cherry tomatoes, cucumber, capers and fresh basil leaves, torn into small pieces, into the bowl.

Separately, in a small bowl, whisk together olive oil and wine vinegar, with lots of sea salt and freshly ground pepper. Toss everything well and serve.

TUSCAN WHITE BEANS WITH SHRIMP

In Tuscany, beans are more than just "poor man's meat"; they are a whole way of life. An excellent source of protein, beans and legumes are low in fat, a great source of fiber and rich in antioxidants. This simple preparation is my favorite way to prepare *fagioli* from Tuscany, drizzled with your best olive oil, or peppery arugula vinaigrette and topped with quickly sautéed shrimp.

4 SERVINGS

4 cloves garlic, sliced

2 tablespoons olive oil

½ teaspoon red chili flakes

½ cup Roma tomatoes, seeded and chopped

1 cup fresh basil leaves, chopped

1 tablespoon white wine

sea salt and freshly ground pepper

3 cups cooked cannellini beans

4 tablespoons good quality olive oil

16 large shrimp (about 1 lb), peeled and deveined

½ cup arugula vinaigrette

FOR ARUGULA VINAIGRETTE

2 cups arugula leaves, washed and dried

½ shallot, sliced

2 teaspoons Dijon mustard

2 tablespoons lemon juice

2 tablespoons red wine vinegar

½ cup good quality olive oil

sea salt and pepper to taste

Preheat a large skillet over medium-high heat, add 2 tablespoons of olive oil and the garlic to the pan, followed by the red chili flakes. Sauté briefly, until the garlic browns slightly.

Add the chopped tomato and basil, stir briefly, then add the white wine. Season with salt and pepper, cook for 1 minute to reduce the wine, then stir in the cooked white beans to reheat.

Keep warm.

Heat 4 tablespoons olive oil in a medium skillet over high heat. Add the shrimp, season with salt and cook about 1 minute, tossing frequently. Once cooked, spoon the warm beans onto a platter or individual plates, drizzle with arugula vinaigrette, top with the warm shrimp and serve.

Combine all the ingredients for the arugula vinaigrette in a blender and process on high for 30 seconds. Check for seasoning with salt and pepper to taste. Store in a glass jar in refrigerator if making ahead and shake well before using. Makes 1 cup.

ARTICHOKES, FRESH PEAS AND FAVA BEANS

Use hand-picked artichokes from the farmers market,
or good quality store-bought artichokes in oil. This is a vibrant summery vegetable
offering. Flood the plate with a big spoonful of the vegetables and then drizzle
generously with a good quality lemon-flavored olive oil. Top with slices
of grilled or roasted meats, so the juices and flavors all mingle.

4 SERVINGS

½ cup extra virgin olive oil

2 shallots, finely chopped

1 garlic clove, finely chopped

2 cups vegetable broth
or water

1 tablespoon white vinegar

sea salt and freshly ground
pepper

6 baby artichokes, peeled
of outer leaves, cleaned
and quartered

OR jarred artichoke hearts
in oil, quartered

1 cup fava beans (broad
beans), podded (2 lbs
unpodded)

1 cup fresh peas, shelled,
or frozen peas

½ cup mint leaves, coarsely
chopped

½ cup flat leaf parsley,
coarsely chopped

1 lemon, zested and juiced,
plus extra slices to serve

lemon-flavored olive oil

Heat 2 tablespoons of oil in a large frying pan over medium-high heat. Add shallots and garlic and cook for 2 minutes. Add vegetable broth, vinegar and a large pinch of sea salt, bring to a simmer and add baby artichokes. Reduce heat to low, cover partially with a lid and cook, stirring occasionally, for 10 minutes or until just tender. (If using jarred artichoke hearts, you can omit this step.) Remove the artichokes to a medium bowl and allow to cool.

Next, add the fava beans to the simmering liquid and cook, uncovered, for 2 minutes, then add shelled peas and simmer for 2 minutes more or until beans are tender and bright green. With a slotted spoon, remove the beans and peas to the bowl of artichokes, season with sea salt and pepper and set aside to cool slightly.

Finally, add the fresh chopped herbs, the lemon zest and a squeeze of fresh lemon juice. Spoon onto a serving platter, drizzle with lemon-flavored olive oil and scatter with lemon slices.

CANTUCCINI
ITALIAN ALMOND COOKIES

Essentially *biscotti*, these famous Italian almond cookies are made from scratch in Tuscany. Dry and crunchy, they are typically served with a glass of the very potent digestive liqueur Vin Santo as a nice end to a hearty meal. I think they are just as good with your morning coffee or pot of tea.

MAKES APPROX 3 DOZEN

3 cups all-purpose flour

1 cup granulated sugar, plus more for sprinkling

1 cup whole almonds

2 teaspoons baking powder

2 teaspoons anise seeds

finely grated zest of 1 lemon

¼ teaspoon salt

3 large eggs

2 large egg yolks

2 teaspoons Vin Santo or other sweet wine

1 large egg white, beaten

Preheat the oven to 350°F. Line a baking sheet with parchment paper.

In the bowl of a standing mixer fitted with a paddle, combine the flour with 1 cup of granulated sugar, almonds, baking powder, anise seeds, lemon zest and salt. Add the whole eggs, egg yolks and Vin Santo and beat at low speed until a stiff, crumbly, slightly sticky dough forms.

Turn the dough onto a lightly floured work surface and knead it 2 or 3 times, until it just comes together. Divide the dough into 3 equal pieces and form each one into a log 12 inch x 2 inch. Transfer the logs to the prepared baking sheet. Brush the tops of the logs with the egg white and sprinkle lightly with granulated sugar. Bake in the center of the oven for 25 minutes, or until the logs are lightly browned and slightly firm. Let them cool for 30 minutes on the baking sheet, then transfer to a cutting board.

While the logs are still warm, cut them on a slight angle into 1/2-inch slices with a sharp serrated knife. Arrange the slices cut sides down on 2 baking sheets with parchment paper, and bake, turning once, until golden, about 25 minutes. Once fully cooled, the cantuccini can be stored in an airtight container for up to a week.

HOMEMADE MASCARPONE CHEESE

I just discovered that making mascarpone cheese is easy and much less expensive
than buying it and I must confess that I am addicted. It is fantastic added
to yogurt for a rich and smooth dessert, turned into ice cream,
or added to soups for a touch of creaminess. You will need an instant read
or digital thermometer to make this recipe.

MAKES ABOUT 2 CUPS

2 cups heavy cream
1 tablespoon lemon juice

In a saucepan, slowly bring the heavy cream to a low simmer.
Let simmer at 180°F for about 3 minutes; add the lemon juice.
Simmer for another 3 minutes and remove from heat. Let cool
to room temperature, about 30 minutes. Fill a small strainer
with several layers of cheesecloth or a nut-milk bag and put
a small bowl under the strainer. Pour the cooled mascarpone
mixture into the cheesecloth and leave the entire bowl
in the fridge overnight.

NOTE   Mine only strained a few tablespoons of liquid (whey),
but the mascarpone came out thick and creamy in the morning.
Add to your favorite recipe or store refrigerated in a glass jar
for up to a week.

TASTE
of GREECE

In 1992, when I was 29, I lucked into an opportunity to visit Greece with my very close friend Kristina Livos.

On that inaugural trip to the island of Zakynthos, I was served a stew of rabbit by her friendly family, welcoming me into the village of Pigadakia. Thereafter Kristina's mother Mavra nicknamed me Kouneli, which means little Rabbit or sweet Rabbit—so endearing, as Mavra could not say Robin. We dove into the traditional **Greek dishes** (some are featured in this chapter), which she prepared for us each day after our jaunts to Porto Zoro, our favorite beach.

Mediterranean homes often have two kitchens, preferring to cook outside, especially in the warm summer months.

Mavra prepared all of our meals in her tiny "outside kitchen" even though she had a fully functioning luxurious kitchen inside her home.

I was also introduced to the **mezze** tradition of feasting on small dishes, which has spread throughout the Mediterranean and the Middle East as a casual, companionable way to eat. I laugh literally every time remembering how much **tzatziki** I ate that trip, setting out to try it at every beach-side taverna or casual cafe. Surprisingly, my Greek-born friend hates olives, so I got to eat them all wherever we were served.

The inherent healthfulness of a Greek meal comes with abundant platters of vegetables, riches from the family garden, enhanced with **basil** and **wild oregano**. Fish and seafood are essential to the Greek table—some are grilled and served al fresco. Even today, most Greeks predominantly eat what's grown nearby and practice traditional ways of cooking and eating—the living embodiment of the term locavore.

My **Santorini cocktail** is a shout out to the icy-cold thirst quencher we guzzled in Oia, after our moped rides to the coast to watch the famed sunsets on the northern part of the island of Thira. It certainly was the most beautiful and picturesque village of Santorini. Riding on our scooters back to our bed & breakfast, we giggled the whole way in the hour of dusk, after a full day in the sun.

On the last, unforgettable night of my first trip to Zakynthos, Greece, we were taking a walk after dinner, and devoured a sweet called **fitoura**, prepared to order in the small town square. In my homage to Greece, I've included this recipe as a unique dessert. I will always remember that sweet crisp treat, doused with cinnamon and sugar, served in a small paper bag.

Greece

SANTORINI SUNSET COCKTAIL

For an inventive and delicious cocktail, thyme–infused honey adds
a pronounced floral sweetness and freshly squeezed grapefruit juice is
a must for this refreshing libation.

FOR 2 COCKTAILS

2 slices pink grapefruit

8 mint leaves

4 teaspoons thyme-infused
honey or good local honey

4 oz vodka

6 oz freshly squeezed
pink grapefruit juice

2 oz Campari

In each glass, muddle the grapefruit slices together with mint
and honey. Add vodka, grapefruit juice, and Campari.
Top the glass with ice cubes and gently stir all the contents
together. Garnish with a sprig of thyme.

THYME-INFUSED HONEY

I love how easy infused honey is to make and how many ways you can use it.
My favorite way so far is to sweeten cocktails, or make a few mini jars of thyme honey
for the perfect house warming gift, use in hot or iced tea, or take a spoonful
to soothe coughs naturally.

sprigs of fresh thyme – washed and dried

raw honey – local honey is preferred

Fill a glass jar roughly half full with fresh thyme. The more thyme you use, the stronger the flavor will be. Cover thyme with honey, filled to the top. Stir the herbs a bit to coat them in honey, to remove any air bubbles. Put lid firmly on jar and place in a warm spot, preferably by a sunny window to allow honey to infuse for at least 5 days. The longer you wait, the more flavorful your honey will be. (If you need a faster method you can put the honey and thyme in a double boiler. Heat at 180°F for 10-15 minutes).

After 5 days, check to see if the honey smells and tastes like thyme. If it does, then you are done! You can strain the thyme out through a cheesecloth before use, but it's messy.
I prefer to just leave the thyme in. Store in a cool cupboard.
Herb-infused honey will last for several months.

SMOKED SALMON TARAMASALATA

A Greek salmon spread, typically made from tarama, the salted and cured fish roe, is an original way to use up leftover smoked salmon and works well on a shared mezze platter. It is also dynamite on toasted bagels.

MAKES 2 CUPS

4 oz smoked salmon

8 oz low-fat mild cheese, cream cheese or ricotta cheese, soft at room temperature

4 oz crème fraîche or sour cream

1 small lemon, juiced

sea salt and freshly ground pepper

extra virgin olive oil, to serve

pitted Kalamata olives and toasted pita bread, to serve

Add smoked salmon, soft cheese, crème fraîche and lemon juice in a food processor. Blend everything until smooth, then stir in sea salt and a large pinch of pepper to taste.

Spoon onto a serving plate, drizzle with olive oil and serve with olives and toasted pita.

POTATO SKORDALIA
WITH VEGETABLE CRUDO

Hailing from Greece, and thick with pureed garlic, olive oil, almonds, and potatoes,
skordalia is particularly delicious with roasted and raw vegetables or,
even better, as an accompaniment to fish.

MAKES 2 CUPS

2 medium russet potatoes,
   peeled and cut into 1-inch
   cubes

sea salt, to taste

½ cup finely ground
   almond meal

8 cloves fresh garlic, smashed
   and minced into a paste

1 cup extra virgin olive oil

2 tablespoons red wine
   vinegar or lemon juice

Place cut potatoes into a 2-qt. saucepan with cold water to cover.
Season with salt and bring to a boil. Reduce the heat and simmer
until the potatoes are just tender, about 15 minutes. Be careful
not to overcook them or they can become waterlogged. Saving
some of the cooking liquid, drain the potatoes and transfer
to a medium bowl. Do not rinse with cold water.

Skordalia should be smooth, so mash potatoes well, or push
cooked potatoes through a medium sieve with the back
of a spoon, then stir in almond meal and minced garlic.
Whisk in the olive oil and vinegar (or lemon juice).
Season with salt to taste and if it is a bit too thick, thin
with some of the cooking liquid to loosen the mixture.
It should be the consistency of hummus. Skordalia will keep,
covered and refrigerated, for up to 4 days.

Hand pick a variety of local vegetables in season. Wash
and cut into slices and spears or slice into thin ribbons using
a mandoline or vegetable peeler and serve the vegetable crudo
with the skordalia.

NOTE   If you have a hard time finding almond meal,
you can easily make your own.
Stir 1 cup of raw whole almonds into a pot of boiling water,
turn off the heat and stir to blanch the almonds for 3-4 minutes.
Drain the almonds and place them on a clean, dry dish towel
to rub the skins off. Allow to cool, then pulse in a food
processor until finely ground. Keep in a covered glass jar
in the refrigerator.

GREAT GREEK RICE SALAD

Greek salad and all of its crunchy, salty, briny goodness is one of my go-to favorite salads.
Served with whole grains and the addition of poached chicken or shrimp,
it makes a refreshing twist on a main course salad with authentic flavor
and may just become one of your favored recipes.

4 SERVINGS

2 cups cooked basmati rice

1 cup grape tomatoes, sliced in half

1 cup cucumber, diced

⅓ cup Kalamata olives, pitted
    and sliced

2 tablespoons capers

2 tablespoons fresh mint, leaves torn

½ cup feta vinaigrette (see below)

sea salt and freshly ground pepper
    to taste

fresh salad greens

1 lemon, cut into wedges

cooked chicken or shrimp

FOR FETA VINAIGRETTE

2 tablespoons red onion, diced

1 clove fresh garlic, peeled

2 tablespoons red wine vinegar

pinch of sugar

pinch of sea salt

freshly ground pepper

1 teaspoon fresh oregano, chopped

2 tablespoons crumbled feta cheese

2 tablespoons good quality olive oil

In a large bowl, gently combine the cooked rice, tomato,
cucumber, olives, capers, fresh mint and half of the feta
vinaigrette. Season with salt and pepper. Arrange fresh
greens on a platter or individual plates and place rice
mixture on top of the greens.

Top with sliced cooked chicken or shrimp, with lemon
wedges and extra feta dressing on the side.

To make the dressing, place all the ingredients in a blender
and process until creamy.

For a more simple dressing, place all the ingredients
chopped or minced into a mason jar and shake until well
blended. Refrigerate for up to 1 week. Makes ½ cup.

GARIDES SAGANAKI
SHRIMP WITH TOMATOES
AND FETA CHEESE

The term saganaki refers to the skillet in which Greeks cook ingredients with cheese.
In this main course, the shrimp is topped with crumbled feta and broiled.

4 SERVINGS

3 tablespoons good quality
   olive oil

4 cloves garlic, minced

4 scallions, minced

½ cup ouzo or white wine

1 teaspoon dried oregano

½ teaspoon sugar

¼ teaspoon red chili flakes

4 medium tomatoes, diced

3 tablespoons chopped fresh
   mint

sea salt and freshly ground
   pepper, to taste

16 large shrimp (about 1 lb),
   peeled and deveined
   or use whole

4 oz feta cheese

1 lemon, halved

1 tablespoon fresh parsley,
   roughly chopped

Heat oil in a 10-inch skillet over medium heat. Add garlic
and scallions and saute until soft, 3-4 minutes. Stir in ouzo
or wine and cook until reduced by half, 3-4 minutes.
Stir in dried oregano, sugar, red chili flakes, and diced tomatoes.
Reduce heat to medium-low and simmer, stirring often,
until slightly thickened, about 6-10 minutes. Stir in the fresh
mint and season with salt and pepper, to taste.

Under a preheated broiler, or on a hot barbeque or stove top grill
pan, grill the shrimp until pink and cooked through.
Arrange the shrimp in a heat proof casserole dish, pour the spiced
tomato mixture over the shrimp, and crumble feta over top.
Broil until bubbly, on the rack closest to the top, for 3-5 minutes.
Squeeze fresh lemon on top and garnish with parsley.

SOUVLAKI WITH LADOLEMONO

Tender cuts of meat marinated in a lemony olive oil mixture create this Greek specialty. Fresh oregano and garlic give these grilled skewers their signature flavor.

2-4 SERVINGS

½ cup ladolemono sauce, see recipe below

¼ cup red wine

1 tablespoon fresh oregano, chopped

6 cloves fresh garlic, minced

1 lb trimmed pork shoulder, cut into 2-inch cubes

4 metal or wooden skewers

sea salt and freshly ground pepper, to taste

lemon wedges, for serving

In a medium bowl, whisk ½ cup of ladolemono sauce (see recipe below) together with the red wine, fresh oregano and freshly minced garlic. Add cubes of pork and toss to coat.
Cover and refrigerate for at least 1 hour or overnight. Meanwhile, if using wooden skewers, soak in warm water.

Build a medium-hot fire in a charcoal grill or heat a gas grill to medium high. Thread about 4-5 pieces of pork onto each skewer so that pork pieces just touch each other.
Season with salt and pepper and discard any leftover marinade. Transfer the skewered meat to the grill. Cook, turning often, until cooked through and slightly charred, about 10 minutes. Serve with lemon wedges and extra ladolemono sauce drizzled over. (Do not use the leftover sauce from marinating the raw pork.)

LADOLEMONO

The Greek version of lemon sauce, is like a supercharged vinaigrette. It's a natural partner to grilled meats and seafood.

2-4 SERVINGS

½ cup fresh lemon juice

2 tablespoons Dijon mustard

1 tablespoon dried oregano

1 cup extra virgin olive oil

sea salt and freshly ground black pepper, to taste

Whisk together lemon juice, mustard, and oregano in a small bowl. While whisking, slowly pour in the oil and season with salt and pepper.
Whisk before serving, as sauce will separate. To expand on this simple sauce, feel free to add other fresh herbs, capers or chopped shallots.

HONEY YOGURT PARFAIT

For me, nothing says Greece more than Greek yogurt and honey. The addition of mascarpone makes this extra rich and creamy and using 0% nonfat yogurt makes this treat sinful without the added fat.

4 SERVINGS

2 cups Greek nonfat plain
yogurt

1 cup mascarpone

zest 1 lemon

zest 1 orange

¾ cup thyme-infused honey,
see page 109

sliced almonds or walnuts

fresh fruit or berries, tossed
with a splash of orange
blossom water

Strain the yogurt in a fine mesh strainer and place over a bowl for 2 hours (or overnight). Reserve the liquid whey for another use.

Stir together the yogurt "cheese" and mascarpone with the lemon and orange zests, then stir in about ½ cup of the honey, reserving about 4 tablespoons for the top.

This can be kept in the fridge for up to 7 days.

To serve, dish the yogurt into individual servings, scatter with nuts, drizzle the remaining honey over the yogurt, and top with sliced fruit or berries, tossed with the orange blossom water.

FITOURA
TRADITIONAL SEMOLINA SWEET

The traditional semolina sweet of Zakynthos served at all the celebrations on the island, especially on the celebration of Agios Dionisios. This recipe makes more than 4 dozen pieces; reduce the recipe in half for a smaller batch.

MAKES 4 DOZEN

6 cups water

¼ teaspoon salt

2 cups thick semolina

sugar and cinnamon
   to garnish

1 cup olive oil for frying,
   plus extra for pan

Lightly oil a 9 x12-inch pan.

Place a large pot of water to boil with salt. When boiling, add semolina, little by little, while stirring constantly with a long wooden spoon until the mixture is combined and thick like polenta.

Pour the semolina mixture into the oiled pan. Spread it out with a spatula to smooth the surface. After a few hours, when the dough is cool, use a knife to cut rectangular or diamond-shaped pieces.

Have ready the sugar and cinnamon in a medium bowl.

In a medium frying pan, with a little olive oil, in batches, add the pieces and fry them on both sides. Be careful not to use too much oil, just add a bit when needed. Once the fitoura have a nice crust all over, drain the pieces onto a paper towel and then toss them into the sugar and cinnamon.

Serve warm.

TASTE
of MIDDLE EAST

My traveling partner's mother would have an entire spread prepared and ready to be devoured by the whole family each day by two in the afternoon. **Labneh**—the homemade yogurt cheese—thick and creamy, topped with a generous dose of golden olive oil and **za'atar spice**. Plump dates, homemade pickles and glistening bowls of black olives adorned the table.

A warm aromatic bread loaf from the baker down the street sits covered with a pretty cloth, and in the middle of it at all, the main attraction, a large pan of green **shakshuka**, its nests of eggs and garden greens interspersed with salty bites of feta. Ah yes, and warm turmeric tea, **date-filled cookies** and sweet halva, made from pressed sesame paste scattered with nuts. Visiting this far off land

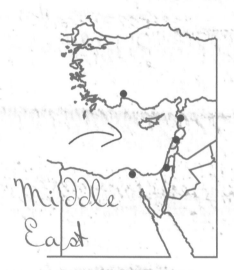

with my friend raised in this region, these are the memories of my first journey to the Middle East. This Mediterranean region, influenced by ancient Israel and nearby Turkey, Syria, Lebanon, and Egypt offers much cultural diversity and the abundance of freshly grown fruits and vegetables, much like the Santa Barbara coast. The warmth of the summer heat invading the veranda, morning swims and early evening dunks in the **Mediterranean Sea** just across the street was the routine for the weeks I spent in a country so foreign yet so familiar. Exploring the fragrant food stalls in the market and spice shops became my obsession. I spent hours searching out the best **falafel**, the tastiest spice blends and the most unique kitchen gadget. I have a strong connection to Israel, the people, the land and especially the cuisine. Middle Eastern style of cooking is very close to my heart, maybe because the combinations of spices are expressed in such a relaxed, intimate way. Middle Eastern dishes aren't just foods that you buy on the street for a late-night snack. They are easy to make at home with the right ingredients, an invitation to try these delicious foods bursting with flavor.

TURMERIC PINEAPPLE COCKTAIL

The pineapple juice is refreshing on its own. In this cocktail, the sweetness of the pineapple is mellowed out by the cucumber and invigorated with the fresh turmeric. The pineapple-turmeric juice has anti-inflamatory properties and enzymes that aid in digestion, making this a perfect aperitif.

FOR 2 COCKTAILS

1 pineapple, peeled, core removed, cut into thin wedges

2 cucumbers, peeled and cut into thin strips

2-inch piece of fresh turmeric root or 1 teaspoon dry turmeric

FOR THE DRINK

8 oz pineapple turmeric juice, chilled

4 oz bourbon

Cointreau or Triple Sec

Juice the pineapple, cucumber, and turmeric. If you have a masticating juicer, the juice will keep for 3 full days.

Combine cold pineapple turmeric juice with bourbon and a splash of orange liqueur and pour into chilled glasses. Do not dilute with ice.

BOREKAS

These crisp handmade phyllo rolls filled with lamb, currants and pine nuts and served with yogurt are a traditional street food in many Middle Eastern neighborhoods. Borekas are typically made with a rich puff pastry, filled with potatoes, cheese or meat, or—for a sweet version—use various fruits and nuts. This lamb-filled variety has been "reinvented" and lightened up using phyllo pastry, slightly sweetened with currants and tossed with toasted almonds.

MAKES 12 BOREKAS

1 large onion, chopped

1 tablespoon olive oil

1 lb ground lamb or beef (mix of both, if you prefer)

½ teaspoon allspice

1 teaspoon sweet paprika

1 teaspoon cinnamon

¼ cup dried currants

sea salt and freshly ground pepper

2 tablespoons chopped parsley

½ cup almonds, toasted

1 cup good quality olive oil for brushing phyllo

phyllo pastry (12 sheets)

Remove phyllo from the fridge for two hours or thaw frozen phyllo in the fridge overnight before using

In a medium sauté pan, cook the onion in olive oil over medium-high heat until softened. Add the ground meat and stir fry until cooked through, breaking the meat up with a wooden spoon to keep it minced. Remove from heat into a medium bowl and stir in spices, currants and a generous sprinkling of salt, pepper and chopped parsley. Allow to cool.

Toast the nuts and roughly chop.

Open the packet of phyllo, carefully unroll and take out 12 sheets. Cover them with a dry tea towel and then with a damp tea towel. Keep the phyllo covered as you work to stop it from becoming dry and brittle. Roll up the remaining unused pastry and return to the fridge.

Lay one sheet of phyllo lengthwise in front of you on a dry work surface. Brush about a tablespoon of olive oil all over the phyllo with a pastry brush.

Preheat the oven to 350°F.

Working quickly, add a few spoonfuls of the filling in the center bottom quarter of the sheet and spread it out 6 inches along the length of the dough. Fold in each side of the dough to cover the filling and brush with a bit more olive oil and roll up from the bottom forming a cigar-filled shape. Fill the remaining phyllo sheets and place each one to line up on an oiled baking tray an inch apart from each other.

Bake the borekas for about 30 minutes until golden brown. Remove from the oven and carefully arrange on your serving platter with the toasted nuts and a drizzle of yogurt.

MANAKESH ZA'ATAR FLAT BREAD

In a pinch, you can use store-bought flatbreads or even pizza dough, but it's really worth the effort to make your own dough. I love the touch of olive oil in it, and kneading the soft dough is a therapeutic experience. Baked briefly in the oven, the manakesh turn chewy and crispy.

4 SERVINGS

3 ½ cups all-purpose flour

1 tablespoon sugar

2 teaspoons sea salt

1 teaspoon instant yeast

2 tablespoons good quality olive oil

1 ½ cups lukewarm water

8 tablespoons za'atar spice blend - see page 143

8 tablespoons good quality olive oil

In a large bowl, mix dry ingredients together, then stir in olive oil and lukewarm water. Be careful not to use hot water (you do not want to kill the yeast). Stir together to form a rough ball, then turn out onto a floured work surface and knead the dough briefly to form a smooth ball of dough. You do not have to knead longer than a few minutes.

Put the dough back into the bowl, sprinkle with a small amount of flour and cover with a clean dry towel. Place in a warm spot to rise for about 1½ hours until double in size.

While the dough is rising, mix the za'atar spice with the olive oil to form a paste and set aside.

Preheat oven to 400°F. Divide dough into four pieces and roll each piece into a long rectangular shape, roughly 12 inches long by 6 inches wide.

Place onto an oiled baking sheet and spread a few tablespoons of the za'atar-oil paste all over. Bake for approximately 5-10 minutes until crisp on the bottom and baked through. Serve warm.

If using as a base for toppings, cool slightly, then spread a few spoonfuls of the preserved lemon labneh (see page 134) on the flat bread, crumble on some smoked salmon or smoked trout and scatter with a few tablespoons of dukkah spice. The combinations are endless.

PRESERVED LEMON LABNEH

Some call it yogurt cheese, others call it Lebanese cream cheese, *labneh* is a creamy, thick DIY yogurt cheese, used as a spread or doctor up a bowlful with olive oil and herbs as a veggie dip. It's very healthy and simple to make.

MAKES 2 CUPS

1 quart Greek nonfat yogurt

2 tablespoons of pureed
    preserved lemon

sea salt and pepper

Line a colander with clean cheesecloth or a double layer of paper towels. Scoop your 32-oz container of Greek yogurt onto the cloth and fold the cloth over the yogurt to cover.

Place the colander in a large bowl to catch the whey in a small saucer underneath so the bottom of the colander is slightly lifted and not sitting in the liquid. Allow to drain in the refrigerator overnight. The next day, transfer to a lidded glass container and refrigerate for up to 2 weeks. Save the liquid whey in a separate glass container for other uses. Now that you have this simple base, you can flavor the labneh with pureed preserved lemon and generously season with salt and pepper, or flavor it according to the dish you are making with fresh herbs and spices.

GREEN SHAKSHUKA

Traditionally made with red sauce, a slightly different take on a traditional Middle Eastern breakfast dish, this savory green shakshuka is a perfect way to celebrate your garden greens. Served as a first course or brunch, this colorful dish will never disappoint.

4 SERVINGS

1 bunch leeks (about 2 cups), thinly sliced and washed

2 tablespoons olive oil

3 garlic cloves, peeled and sliced

6 cups mixed kale, swiss chard, and spinach, washed and chopped

½ cup fresh cilantro, chopped

¼ cup fresh dill, chopped

¼ cup fresh oregano, chopped

1 teaspoon red chili flakes

pinch of nutmeg

1 teaspoon sea salt and freshly ground pepper

¼ cup yogurt

6 eggs

½ cup crumbled feta cheese

Shake the water off the leeks and saute in a medium cast iron skillet or saute pan in the olive oil until translucent, about 10 minutes. Add the sliced garlic and cook an additional minute. Stir in the chopped greens and cook until leaves are wilted, about 4-5 minutes, stirring occasionally.

Add in the fresh chopped herbs and red chili flakes, nutmeg, and salt and pepper to season. Stir in the yogurt to combine.

Create 6 nests, and break an egg into each, stirring the egg whites slightly into the green mixture. Cook on medium-low heat for an additional 3-5 minutes, covered or until eggs are done to your liking. Top with crumbled feta cheese and serve immediately.

FALAFEL CHICKEN

A few years ago, I visited the Middle East for the first time. While writing
in my cookbook journal, among other things, I was obsessed with eating falafel,
the very popular street food, typically made from garbanzo beans or chickpeas.
From that, I've created my gluten-free "breading" for chicken using these same exotic
flavors of pairing fried chicken and falafel. The mixture goes really well with fish too.
Serve with a simple shepherd's salad of tomato, cucumber,
onion and parsley and tehina sauce.

4 SERVINGS

4 cups garbanzo bean flour

2 tablespoons sea salt

1 tablespoon each of ground
  cumin, garlic powder and
  smoked paprika

2 teaspoons ground coriander

2 teaspoons turmeric powder

¼ teaspoon cayenne pepper

2 teaspoons sea salt

½ teaspoon freshly ground
  pepper

2 tablespoons sesame seeds

2 eggs

1 tablespoon Dijon mustard

4 large boneless and skinless
  chicken breasts
  or 8 boneless skinless
  chicken thighs

olive oil

tehina sauce - see page 140

Blend the dry garbanzo bean flour with the salt, all the spices
and sesame seeds to prepare the falafel coating and set
in a shallow pan.

Whisk the eggs and mustard in a medium bowl and place
chicken in to cover.

Remove the chicken from the egg mixture and coat
with the falafel mix, shaking off any excess.

(Save any leftover falafel seasoning in a plastic bag in the freezer.
The mix can be used over again for another meal; it's very
important to mark it as "Use with chicken only.")

Heat about ½ inch of olive oil in a large, heavy skillet over
medium-high heat. Carefully place the chicken in the hot oil,
taking care not to crowd the pan. Turn the heat to medium
and cook until nicely browned, turning once, 3-4 minutes
per side. Transfer the chicken to an oven safe pan. Bake at 375°F
until firm and cooked through, about 10 minutes.
Arrange chicken on a platter, serve with shepherd's salad,
and drizzle generously with tehina sauce. Don't toss any
leftovers! Save them and cut the chicken up into a salad,
or fold up into a pita or tortilla for a quick snack.

TEHINA SAUCE

The delicious and healthy Mediterranean food of Israel is diverse. In Israel
and the Middle East this sauce is called tehina. It is made from 100% sesame seed
and is used in many different ways, not only limited to hummus, falafel and shawarma.
Just mix in these ingredients and once made into the sauce, it's a near-perfect
substitute as a dressing for chicken or tuna salad instead of mayonaisse.
Mix the sesame paste with a little bit of honey and cinnamon for toast;
it also adds great texture and nutrients to guacamole and smoothies.

MAKES ¾ CUP

½ cup tahini paste
3-5 tablespoons warm water
1 lemon, cut in half
sea salt
cayenne pepper

In a small bowl, blend tahini paste with 3 tablespoons of warm water with a fork until smooth. Add the juice of half a lemon and season with salt to taste and a dash of cayenne pepper (optional). Taste and adjust the consistency with a little more water or lemon juice as needed. Any of the following can be added for extra flavor—fresh chopped garlic, chopped parsley or cilantro. Refrigerate for up to 1 week.

SHEPHERD'S SALAD

A favorite in Turkey, where fresh tomatoes and cucumbers are sweet and plentiful during the summer months, this salad is popular in many Middle Eastern countries. Delicious and healthy, and serves as a favored accompaniment to the Falafel Chicken.

4 SERVINGS

1 clove fresh garlic, peeled and chopped

¼ cup fresh lemon juice or wine vinegar

¼ cup good quality olive oil

pinch of sea salt and freshly ground pepper

1 teaspoon dry mint or 2 sprigs of fresh mint

6 Persian cucumbers, diced small (the idea is to use seedless cucumbers)

2 cups tomatoes, diced small

½ cup red onion, diced small

capers, optional

Put the dressing ingredients in a small mason jar, cover and shake them together to mix thoroughly. Taste the dressing and adjust the flavor to suit you—it may need a splash more vinegar, or a little extra salt—then set the jar aside and cut the vegetables.

Combine all the diced vegetables. Add some of the dressing to lightly coat and gently toss together. Cover and place in the fridge for 20 minutes. Check seasoning and garnish the salad with capers, sliced radishes, chopped bell pepper or pomegranate arils to jazz it up.

ZA'ATAR SPICE BLEND

Za'atar adds a bright flavor to salads, stirred into olive oil and brushed onto flat breads or mixed with your best marinade for chicken, fish, and red meats.

MAKES 1 CUP

¼ cup sumac

2 tablespoons dried thyme

1 tablespoon roasted sesame seeds

2 tablespoons dried marjoram

2 tablespoons dried oregano

1 teaspoon sea salt

Mix all of the ingredients by pulsing in a food processor; do not overmix—the sesame seeds should still be recognizable.
A mortar and pestle will work fine too. Store the spice in a glass container with a tight lid and keep the container in a cool dark place. The freshness will last for several months.

DUKKAH SPICE BLEND

Dukkah is a crumbly nut and spice blend from Egypt. It's really good on roasted vegetables, potatoes, sprinkled on soups and in salads.

MAKES 1 CUP

½ cup toasted pistachios

¼ cup coriander seeds

3 tablespoons sesame seeds

2 tablespoons cumin seeds

1 teaspoon fennel seeds

1 tablespoon black peppercorns

1 teaspoon dried mint leaves

1 teaspoon sea salt

Heat a heavy skillet over medium heat, toast or "dry roast" the spices, drawing out their aroma. Cool completely. Place the nuts and seeds, along with the mint and salt, into a mortar and pound until the mixture is crushed, or pulse in a coffee grinder for a coarse consistency.
Do not allow the mixture to become a paste. Store in an airtight container for 1 month.

CHICKEN SHAWARMA

An oven-roasted version of the classic street food, served on pita with tehina. Pickled cabbage or shepherd's salad, olives, chopped parsley, and feta also make flavorful additions. You can be creative here and use whatever you have on hand.

4 SERVINGS

2 lemons, juiced

½ cup plus 1 tablespoon olive oil

6 cloves garlic, peeled and minced

1 teaspoon sea salt

1 teaspoon freshly ground pepper

2 teaspoons ground cumin

2 teaspoons paprika

½ teaspoon turmeric

pinch ground cinnamon

red pepper flakes, to taste

2 pounds boneless, skinless chicken thighs

2 tablespoons fresh parsley, chopped

Prepare the marinade for the chicken. Combine the lemon juice, ½ cup olive oil, garlic, salt, pepper, cumin, paprika, turmeric, cinnamon and red pepper flakes in a large bowl, and whisk to combine. Add the chicken and toss well to coat. Cover and store in the refrigerator for at least 2 and up to 12 hours.

When ready to cook, preheat the oven to 400°F.
Use the remaining tablespoon of olive oil to oil a rimmed sheet pan. Remove the chicken from the marinade and place on the pan, spreading out evenly. Roast the chicken in the oven until browned, crisp at the edges and cooked through, about 40 minutes. (To make the chicken even crisper, set the pan under the broiler for 5 minutes after roasting.)

Cool slightly, then slice chicken thinly or shred with your fingers. Serve on grilled pita.

KOFTA KEBABS

My Lebanese neighbor introduced me to these years ago.
They have six different kinds of aromatic spices and are made of ground lamb.
After creating and smelling this recipe, I am pretty close to replicating the flavors
and aromas I fondly remember. Of course, if preferred, using ground turkey
instead of lamb is equally delicious.

4 SERVINGS

4 cloves garlic, minced

2 teaspoons sea salt

1 pound ground lamb
or turkey

3 tablespoons grated white
onion

3 tablespoons chopped fresh
parsley

3 tablespoons chopped fresh
cilantro

1 tablespoon ground
coriander

1 tablespoon ground cumin

1 tablespoon ground
cinnamon

1 teaspoon ground allspice

½ teaspoon ground ginger

¼ teaspoon cayenne pepper

12 bamboo skewers, soaked
in water for 30 minutes

Mash the garlic into a paste with the salt using a mortar and
pestle or the flat side of a chef's knife on a cutting board. Mix
the garlic into the ground lamb along with the onion, parsley,
cilantro and six spices in a large mixing bowl until well blended.
Divide the mixture into twelve portions, roll into oval shapes,
rather than round balls, and place on a baking sheet.
Slip a skewer into each oval, pressing to form each kebab around
the bamboo.

Place the kebabs onto a baking sheet, cover, and refrigerate
at least 30 minutes, or can be prepared the day before.

Preheat an outdoor grill on medium heat, and lightly oil
the grates.

Cook the skewers on the preheated grill, turning occasionally,
until the lamb has cooked to your desired degree of doneness,
about 6 minutes for medium. As with many Middle Eastern
foods, serve with yogurt with chopped cucumber and onion.

BAKED RED ONIONS WITH FETA AND WALNUTS

This side dish recipe inspired by Yotam Ottolenghi celebrates the natural sweetness of onion. Red onions are quite sweet and when roasted they taste even more delicious. Try with goat cheese instead of the feta for more intense flavor.

4 SERVINGS

4 medium red onions, peeled

2 tablespoons olive oil

sea salt and freshly ground pepper

handful of parsley leaves, picked

½ cup walnuts, coarsely chopped

1 red chile, finely chopped (optional)

1 garlic clove, peeled and crushed

3 tablespoons red wine vinegar

1 tablespoon olive oil

¼ teaspoon sea salt

½ cup feta cheese, crumbled

Preheat the oven to 400°F. Cut off the tops and bottoms of the onions, slice each onion crossways into 1-inch slices and place in a roasting pan. Brush with olive oil, sprinkle with ¼ teaspoon of salt and some pepper, and roast for 20-30 minutes, until cooked and golden brown on top.

Set aside to cool slightly and place on a serving platter.

While onions are roasting, stir the ingredients together in a small bowl and spoon over the roasted onions. Sprinkle with feta cheese to serve.

SEMOLINA SHORTBREAD

Cinnamon-spiced date-filled shortbread cookies, inspired by Lebanese ma'amoul,
these buttery semolina pastries are scented with rose and orange blossom waters.
The filling is usually either dates or a concoction of walnuts or pistachios.
I have combined all three to create this delicious date-and-nut filling.
Though they are easy to shape by hand, as I have done, it's worth seeking out
a traditional ma'amoul mold to make them.

MAKES ABOUT 2 DOZEN COOKIES

FOR THE CRUST

3 cups fine semolina flour

½ cup almond flour

12 tablespoons unsalted
butter, room temperature,
cut into pieces

3 tablespoons granulated
sugar

½ teaspoon sea salt

⅓ cup whole milk (almond
milk may be substituted)

2 tablespoons rose water

2 teaspoons orange blossom
water

FOR THE FILLING

½ cup walnuts

½ cup shelled pistachios

2 cups pitted dates

8 tablespoons unsalted butter,
cubed and chilled

2 tablespoons ground
cinnamon

½ teaspoon cardamom

Pulse the semolina, almond flour, butter, sugar, and salt in a food
processor until pea-sized crumbles form. Add milk and rose
and orange blossom waters; pulse until dough comes together.
Flatten dough into a disk and wrap in plastic wrap;
chill for 2 hours.

For the filling in a food processor, pulse the nuts first.
Add the pitted dates, butter, cinnamon, and cardamom
and process until smooth. Divide into 24 small balls and chill
for 30 minutes.

Heat oven to 375°F. Divide dough into 24 balls.
Working with 1 ball at a time, press a finger into the dough,
creating a pocket. Place 1 ball of filling into each pocket, pinch
sides to encase the filling and roll into a ball. If you have it,
press the balls into a ma'amoul mold, or flatten slightly using
your palm. Transfer to a baking sheet. Bake until golden,
25-30 minutes. Let cool before serving.

TASTE
of MOROCCO

From my travels in the Mediterranean, there are a few souvenirs I brought back from Morocco. An extremely expensive Berber rug, half a dozen hand-painted Moroccan plates that I still have 15 years later, and, more importantly, memories of the warm aromas of **spices** and the welcoming people, always curious about visitors from America and happy to show them around their village.

Moroccan food, a mix of Mediterranean, Arabic, and Andalusian cuisines, is sensual, exotic and a feast for the eyes. Many of the following recipes were shared with me by my incredibly talented and generous friend, chef Yasmina Ksikes, and are inspired by her grandma Lalla Mina. They are traditional Moroccan recipes with a healthy California twist. Characteristic flavorings include toasted cumin, **cinnamon,** saffron and **preserved lemon**.

As is typical for most Mediterranean cuisines, the staple ingredients include wheat, used for bread and **couscous**, and olive oil. Spices are used extensively in Moroccan foods. Although spices have been imported to Morocco for thousands of years, many ingredients like mint, olives, oranges and lemons are grown there. A classic lunch meal begins with a number of hot and cold salads, possibly **Bastilla**, followed by a **Tagine** with couscous rich with meats and vegetables, and finally, a cup of sweet mint tea, which usually ends the meal. The consumption of alcohol is not common due to religious restrictions. I've included a recipe for a **Mint Mojito** made with a **minted green tea syrup**, which can be made with or without the rum and the recipe for preserved lemon which is used as a salty condiment. Although very different from Santa Barbara, in much of the Mediterranean-Moroccan cuisine, we see similar products prepared in a unique way.

MOROCCAN GREEN TEA MOJITO COCKTAIL

On a hot summer day, the blend of mint leaves, cardamom and green tea is a cool, refreshing libation, made with or without the rum.

MAKES 2 COCKTAILS

1 cup very strongly brewed green tea

1 cup organic sugar

3-4 crushed cardamom pods

4 sprigs fresh mint

2 oz green tea-cardamom simple syrup

2 oz fresh lime juice, plus lime wedges

3 oz white rum, optional

ice cubes

In a small sauce pan, combine the green tea, sugar and cardamom to make the simple syrup. Stir over medium heat until sugar has dissolved. Simmer, stirring occasionally, until reduced by half to create a syrup. This will take about 15 minutes. Strain and allow to cool.

In a cocktail shaker, muddle a few fresh mint leaves, green-tea simple syrup, and fresh lime juice.

Add rum and shake well. Pour into ice-filled glasses and garnish with a fresh sprig of mint and lime wedge.

Multiply the recipe to make a pitcher for a crowd of friends.

TAKTOUKA

You can use a variety of green chiles rather than green bell peppers,
which adds a spicy note to this dish depending on the chiles you use.
You'll need to roast and skin your peppers before you use them in the recipe,
or you can simply use jarred roasted peppers.

4 SERVINGS

1 tablespoon olive oil

2 large ripe tomatoes, diced

2 roasted red peppers, cut
    into julienne strips

2 roasted green peppers,
    cut into julienne strips
    (Anaheim, poblano
    or pasilla)

2 garlic cloves, minced

½ bunch cilantro, chopped

1 tablespoon ground cumin

½ teaspoon smoked paprika

1 teaspoon harissa powder
    or cayenne

1 quarter piece preserved
    lemon rind, finely
    minced - page 176

In a medium sauté pan, on medium heat, add the olive oil
and chopped tomatoes and sauté for a couple of minutes
to soften. Add the pepper strips, garlic, cilantro, spices
and preserved lemon rind.

Stir over medium-high heat for about 10 minutes. Remove from
heat and let stand at room temperature, uncovered. Some of this
mixture will be used as the filling for this savory tart and you
can serve taktouka warm or cold with crusty bread, if desired.
It can be garnished with fresh chopped parsley or cilantro
and a drizzle of olive oil.

SWEET POTATO TAKTOUKA TART

This cheesy and colorful quiche will stand out at your next brunch party. It also works great as a main course for dinner. The tart is very easy to make and tastes rich, although it doesn't include heavy cream or a great deal of cheese. The sliced sweet potato stands in for a crust. If you don't have a mandolin or thin slicing blade, you can use grated sweet potato just as successfully.

4 SERVINGS

1 large sweet potato for the crust, sliced thin or grated

1 tablespoon olive oil

3 large organic eggs

1 ½ cup ricotta

salt and freshly ground pepper to taste

¼ teaspoon smoked paprika

1 ½ cups taktouka

Preheat oven to 350°F.

Put the sweet potato slices (or grated sweet potato) in a bowl and marinate in a tablespoon of olive oil and a pinch of salt and pepper, for 5-10 minutes.

Arrange the sliced or grated sweet potato in a quiche/pie dish and bake in the oven for 15 minutes.

Meanwhile make the tart filling.

In a medium bowl, mix the eggs, 1 cup ricotta, spices and salt and pepper to taste until well blended, then add taktouka and blend together.

Pour the filling over the sweet potato crust, dot the top with the remaining ½ cup of ricotta cheese and bake for 30 more minutes or until all the filling is solid all the way through.

The tart can be flipped onto a serving plate revealing the vibrant sweet potato crust or served warm in the baking dish with more taktouka on the side. Makes a great leftover.

BASTILLA

As it is generously doused with powdered sugar, Morocco's famous chicken pie, masquerades as a dessert until you cut into it. Wonderfully spiced with saffron and cinnamon, the combination of sweet and savory flavors is surprising. Using cooked roasted chicken saves time on preparation. Generally served as a starter, Bastilla makes a nice brunch item served with the Moroccan Carrot Salad featured in this chapter.

8 SERVINGS

8 oz slivered almonds

1 teaspoon cinnamon, plus additional for top of bastilla

⅓ cup powdered sugar, plus additional for top of bastilla

¼ cup butter, plus ¼ cup for brushing on the phyllo dough

1 medium onion, peeled and finely chopped

1 rotisserie cooked chicken (about 3 cups), skin removed, meat taken off bones and shredded

½ teaspoon cinnamon

1 generous pinch saffron

¾ cup chopped fresh parsley

¼ cup chopped fresh cilantro

3 eggs, cracked and beaten with ¼ cup powdered sugar

sea salt and freshly ground pepper, to taste

8 sheets prepared phyllo dough, defrosted in refrigerator for 4 hours or overnight

Heat a large skillet over medium-high heat. Add butter to melt, then add onion and sauté until soft, 4-5 minutes. Add shredded cooked chicken, cinnamon, saffron, parsley, cilantro and salt to taste. Simmer uncovered for 5 minutes, until chicken is heated through. Whisk eggs with the ¼ cup powdered sugar, salt and pepper and mix into the chicken mixture. Stir eggs through for a few minutes, remove from heat and set aside.

Preheat oven to 400°F. Brush a 10-inch spring-form pan with melted butter or cooking spray.

Place 2 phyllo sheets on your work surface to create a very long rectangle, overlapping slightly. Brush with butter and place 2 more sheets on top. Sprinkle with half the almond mixture. Repeat with 2 more phyllo sheets brushing each with butter before adding another 2 sheets. Brush with butter and sprinkle the rest of the almond mixture over the phyllo.

Spoon chicken mixture down the entire length of the phyllo. Fold up into a snake-like roll, and roll it up into a spiral. Place this roll into the buttered pan, and brush the top with more butter. Bake for 35 minutes at 400°F, or until golden. Remove from pan, sprinkle generously with powdered sugar, cinnamon and reserved slivered almonds. Slice into wedges and serve, or, as the Moroccans do, tear it apart and eat with your fingers.

MOROCCAN-STYLE
ROASTED CARROT SALAD

The salad combines both roasted carrots and raw crisp shaved carrot threads.
You'll want to flavor the carrots with the citrus-cumin dressing before roasting
and again while they are still steaming hot.

4 SERVINGS

1 lb carrots, washed,
  not peeled

2 teaspoons whole cumin
  seeds

½ teaspoon red chili flakes

sea salt and freshly ground
  pepper

2 cloves garlic, peeled

extra virgin olive oil

red or white wine vinegar

1 orange, halved

1 lemon, halved

3 ripe avocados

2 handfuls mixed salad leaves
  (arugula or radicchio),
  washed and dried

Preheat oven to 400°F and place all but two carrots
on a roasting tray.

With a mortar and pestle smash up the cumin seeds, red chili
flakes, and a generous pinch of both salt and pepper. Add the
garlic and smash up again until you have a paste. Add enough
extra virgin olive oil to generously cover the paste, and pour
in a shot of vinegar. This mixture will double as a marinade
and a dressing. Stir this all together, then drizzle the marinade
over the carrots in the tray, coating them well. Add the orange
and lemon halves to the tray, cut side down. These will roast
along with the carrots, and their juice will be used as the
dressing. Place in the preheated oven for 30 minutes, or until
charred.

While the carrots are roasting, shave the two reserved raw
carrots into thin threads with a peeler or on a mandolin into
a big mixing bowl. Halve and scoop out the avocados,
cut them into wedges lengthwise and place in the bowl. Remove
the roasted carrots from the oven and add them to the avocados.
Carefully, using tongs, squeeze the juice from the roasted orange
and lemon into a small bowl and add the same amount of extra
virgin olive oil and a little shot of red wine vinegar. Season
with a generous pinch of both salt and pepper, stir together
and pour this dressing over the carrots and avocados.
Add the washed greens, and mix together gently with your hands
or wooden mixing spoons and serve.

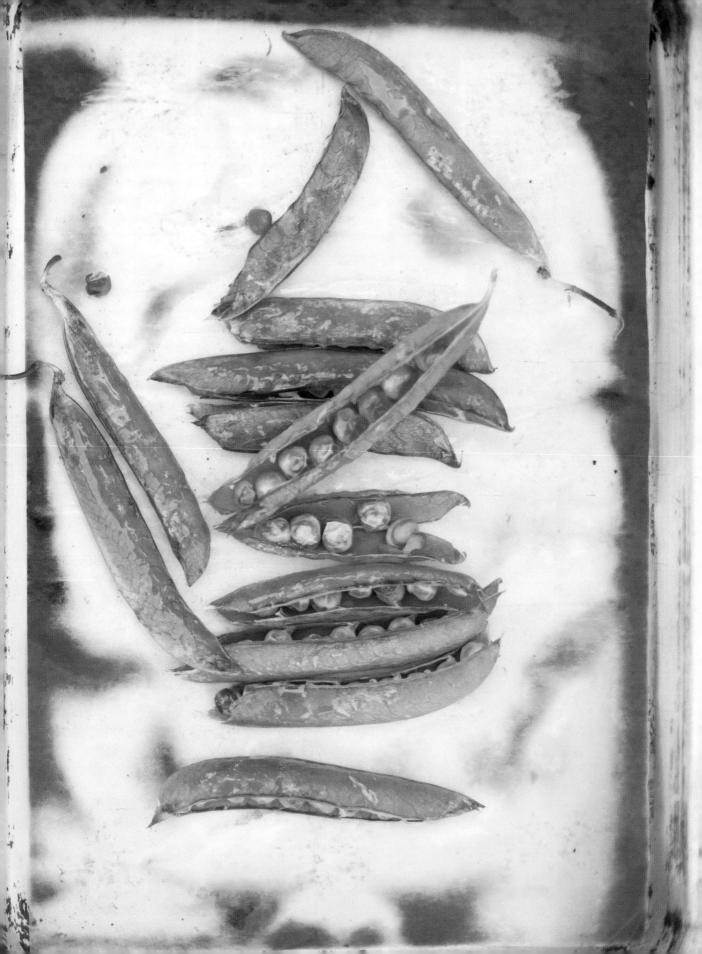

ZAALOUK
MOROCCAN RATATOUILLE

A tasty salad of cooked eggplant, tomatoes, garlic, olive oil and spices bursting
with flavor, this is a common side dish in Morocco, usually served with crusty bread.
Roasting the eggplant eliminates the need to salt the vegetable as typically done
for cooking eggplant and uses much less oil in the recipe.
Include this dish as part of a mezze spread.

4 SERVINGS

1 roasted eggplant - follow directions below for roasting in the oven

2 tablespoons olive oil

2 medium tomatoes, diced (or 4 whole peeled canned tomatoes, diced)

4 garlic cloves, minced

½ cup parsley, chopped

1 quarter preserved lemon, rind chopped

1 teaspoon cumin

1 teaspoon paprika

1 teaspoon harissa paste or spice blend

sea salt and fresh ground pepper

In a medium sauté pan, heat the olive oil, add diced tomatoes and sauté on medium heat for 5 minutes to soften.
Add the minced garlic and half of the chopped parsley, preserved lemon rind and spices. Season to taste with salt and pepper.

Continue cooking another 5 minutes to combine the flavors. Add roasted diced eggplant to combine, sautéing for about 5 minutes. Remove from heat once the eggplant is really tender. Garnish with the rest of the chopped parsley.

NOTE Eggplant can be fire roasted directly over an open flame on your gas stovetop, cooked on an outdoor grill, or roasted under an oven broiler. I find the oven broiler method, as described below, to be the least messy.
Rub 1 teaspoon of olive oil on the eggplant so it will not dry out while cooking. Place the eggplant on a baking sheet on the rack closest to the broiler and turn frequently until the eggplant is evenly charred and the flesh is soft and mushy, about 20 minutes. Remove from the heat and let cool. Cut in half, scoop out the flesh, and chop.

CHERMOULA

A North African sauce traditionally paired with fish, chermoula is a delicious mix
of fresh herbs, earthy spices, and acidic preserved lemon.
I think it's fantastic with other dishes as well and I like to stir spoonfuls
of this pungent sauce into soups, couscous or adding it to chicken.

MAKES 1 CUP

1 teaspoon cumin seeds

½ cup coarsely chopped
 flat-leaf parsley

½ cup coarsely chopped
 cilantro leaves and tender
 stems

3 cloves garlic, peeled
 and chopped

1 teaspoon smoked paprika

2 tablespoons preserved
 lemon rind chopped
 or 1-2 teaspoons fresh
 lemon juice

½ cup olive oil

1 teaspoon chili paste
 (or 1 teaspoon harissa
 spice blend)

sea salt

Sprinkle the cumin seeds in a skillet and toast them over medium
to high heat, stirring, until they smell fragrant, 1-2 minutes.
Set aside.

In the bowl of a food processor (or in a mortar and pestle), place
the parsley, cilantro, garlic, smoked paprika, preserved lemon,
olive oil, chili paste, and toasted cumin. Blend or grind until
smooth.

Taste and add some of the preserved lemon juice. Add salt
to taste. Preserved lemons are salty so be sure to check
for seasoning. Add more olive oil, if necessary, until the sauce
becomes a loose paste.

Store chermoula covered, in a non-reactive glass container.
It will keep in the refrigerator for up to a week.

Use chermoula as a marinade on fish, chicken or seafood,
and toss onto vegetables before roasting or grilling.

CHICKEN TAGINE
WITH ARTICHOKE HEARTS

Tagine is historically a slow-cooked North African dish that is named
after the earthenware pot in which it is cooked. My version takes out the long hours
of cooking. The chicken is simmered in a warming spiced broth with no added fat
or oils, allowing you to savor this fragrant dish guilt free in just under an hour.

4-6 SERVINGS

1 quart chicken broth

2 garlic cloves

½ teaspoon turmeric

1 teaspoon dried ground
    ginger

1 teaspoon saffron threads

2 teaspoons ground coriander

½ teaspoon smoked paprika

1 teaspoon sea salt

4 large organic chicken
    breasts OR 6 chicken
    thighs, both boneless
    and skinless

8 small new potatoes, sliced
    into ½-inch slices

2 tablespoons preserved
    lemon peel (about half
    a lemon), finely chopped

1 14-oz can artichoke
    bottoms, quartered

1 cup fresh shelled
    or frozen peas

½ cup fresh parsley, chopped

6 sprigs of cilantro, chopped

In a large sauce pot, bring the chicken broth with all the spices
and salt to a boil.

Cut chicken breasts into large chunks, or chicken thighs into
quarters, add to the broth and reduce the heat to a medium
simmer for 10 minutes to poach the chicken until just cooked
through. Remove the chicken to a plate and set aside.

Add sliced potatoes and chopped preserved lemon to the broth
and cook for 10-12 minutes on medium heat until just tender.

Add the reserved chicken back into the pot, with the quartered
artichoke bottoms, and heat through for 5 minutes.

Scatter the peas, parsley and cilantro and stir into the stew
to heat the peas through for a few minutes just before serving.
Serve with couscous, noodles or simply prepared rice.

SWEET COUSCOUS WITH CARAMELIZED ONIONS RAISINS AND CINNAMON

The real deal couscous is traditionally cooked in a couscoussière, which looks like a large steamer. Veggies and meats go in the bottom pot, and the couscous goes into the perforated basket on top to be steamed as the main dish cooks under it. I buy the instant couscous, the kind that you add boiling water to, wait 5 minutes and voilà, instant gratification. It's a nice change from rice or pasta, and there are countless flavor combinations. The following is a nice compliment to the Chicken Tagine.

4-6 SERVINGS

1 ½ cup chicken broth
  or water

¼ teaspoon saffron
  or turmeric

1 cup instant couscous

½ cup golden raisins

2 tablespoon olive oil

½ teaspoon cinnamon

sea salt and freshly ground
  pepper to taste

1 cup caramelized onions
  for garnish - see page 59

In a small saucepan, bring the chicken broth and saffron or turmeric to a boil.

Place the couscous and the raisins in a medium bowl seasoned with cinnamon, olive oil and salt and pepper.

Add the boiling broth to couscous, mix, cover and let stand for 10 minutes. After 10 minutes, fluff the couscous with a fork, check seasoning and add salt and pepper to taste. Serve warm with caramelized onions on top or at room temperature.

PRESERVED LEMONS

This recipe combines both salt and sugar, making these preserves versatile
in many dishes, both sweet and savory. A special preserving process requires making
a brine, which is not unlike pickling and takes a bit of time. After ingredients are
combined, they are left to loosen up to transform. Once you've *preserved lemons*,
it's the rind, not the juice or pulp, that you'll be using in most recipes.
After a few weeks you will have something that adds brilliance to dressings,
Moroccan tagines, or even a Bloody Mary.

MAKES 1 QUART

6 organic lemons

½ cup sugar

½ cup kosher salt

1 teaspoon crushed coriander seeds

¼ teaspoon turmeric

3 cloves

Set a large pot of water on the stove and bring to a boil.

Scrub lemons well and place into boiling water for 10 minutes.

With a slotted spoon, transfer lemons to an ice bath (a medium bowl filled with half ice and half cold water). Reserve 2 cups of the cooking liquid.

Mix sugar, salt, coriander seeds, turmeric, and cloves in a small bowl.

Score the lemons by cutting each into quarters but not all the way through to the other end.

In a large bowl add the lemons with the sugar, salt, and spices from the small bowl.

Place the lemons in a clean 1-quart Mason jar. Sprinkle with any remaining sugar-salt-spice mixture, pour reserved cooking liquid in and cover, completely pushing the lemons down with a wooden spoon to totally immerse them in the liquid. Cover with a lid and chill for 2 weeks in the refrigerator.

Once the lemons are preserved, many recipes call for using only the rind and discarding the membrane. I often use the whole lemon. When you remove a lemon from the brining liquid, push the seeds out with your fingers. Chop or puree the whole preserved lemon and add to your preparation.

MOROCCAN CREPES WITH ORANGE BLOSSOM BROWN BUTTER

When I was growing up, my grandmother would get up early and make us crepes for breakfast; a little sticky and sweet, drizzled with honey and sprinkled with chopped toasted almonds. When Yasmina shared with me her grandmother's recipe for baghrir, I recognized these as our breakfast crepes from long ago. These are a welcome light dessert or a great addition to a Sunday brunch, with a big pot of fresh mint tea.

4 SERVINGS

FOR THE CREPES

1 cup water

1 ½ teaspoons instant yeast

1 cup fine semolina flour

pinch of salt

pinch of sugar

2 teaspoons orange blossom
water

FOR THE SAUCE

4 tablespoons unsalted butter

2 tablespoons honey

1 teaspoon cinnamon

1 tablespoon orange blossom
water

½ cup toasted almonds
or sesame seeds for
the topping

Mix just a ½ cup lukewarm water, yeast, and a pinch of sugar together to dissolve the yeast and allow to sit for 5 minutes. In a blender, mix other ½ cup water, semolina flour, salt, orange blossom water and the yeast mixture and blend for about 10 seconds. Let stand for 5-10 minutes.

In a small or medium nonstick pan make your crepes. Heat the pan over medium heat, pouring ¼-½ cup of the batter, tipping the pan around to spread. The batter should have lots of tiny holes. Quickly remove the pan from the heat as soon as the holes finish forming. Cook on one side only; do not flip. Remove to a serving plate.

In the same pan, after making the crepes, melt the butter over medium heat, swirling the butter around to brown it slightly. Add in the honey, cinnamon and orange blossom water and swirl again to combine.

Pour over your crepes and sprinkle with toasted almonds or sesame seeds on top. Serve warm.

INSPIRATIONAL MENUS
FOR ENTERTAINING & PARTIES

MOTHER'S DAY BRUNCH

Everyone knows that Mother's Day is all about brunch. Show your mom you really appreciate everything she's done for you, with this authentic egg dish accompanied by an easy fix salmon platter and baked cherry and custard dessert. If you are rushing about, use the dishwasher as a hiding spot for dirty pots, even those you'll ultimately wash by hand.

Sgroppino al Limone Cocktail
Green Shakshuka
Platter of Smoked Salmon
Simple Butter Lettuce Salad
Cherry Clafouti

BRIDAL SHOWER LADIES LUNCHEON

Honor the bride-to-be with an elegant lunch with this Mediterranean coastal menu. Welcome help from your friends and reserve the small jobs for early birds. Offer the tasks to those who ask, "What can I do to help?" Let them set out the dishes and silverware, plate hors d'oeuvres, and help pour drinks. Champagne after the meal is a nice surprise. It's one of those delightful little touches that people remember. Sit back and relax while opening up gifts and passing around the chocolate.

Turmeric Pineapple Cocktail
Potato Skordalia with Vegetable Crudo
Gazpacho Andaluz
Salmon Niçoise
Warm Bread and Crackers
Chocolate Pistachio Brittle Bark

SIMPLE SUNDAY FAMILY DINNER

Enjoy this well-rounded quick meal with family and friends celebrating the end of a great week. Set the scene for an easy ooh-factor, using a white tablecloth, white dishes and just one or two accent colors with linen napkins. Flowers should be simple and short enough to talk over. Savor any leftovers for a quick weeknight heat up.

Chicken Tagine
Sweet Couscous
Roasted Broccoli with Lemon
Ice Cream

ENGAGEMENT CELEBRATION WITH TAPAS AND COCKTAILS

Deliver a mix of tastes from the Mediterranean, starting with small bites that can all be made early that day and served with cocktails. Have drinks ready in pitchers on a cart or small table and give arriving guests a clear destination. It frees you to scurry back to the kitchen as needed. Follow with platters of skewered meats and seafood for more filling fare that can be cooked in advance and popped in the oven for just minutes to reheat.

Sangría and Santorini Sunrise Cocktail
Butternut Squash Empanadas
Crostini di Prosciutto
Albondigas
Tortillitas de Camarones
Chicken Skewers with Romesco Sauce
Shrimp Skewers with Chermoula Sauce
Kofta Kebabs
Celebration Cake or Cupcakes

SANTA BARBARA BOWL

A trio of salads, along with a few spreads and dips, can be made in advance and packed in lightweight, non-breakable containers, tucked inside a sturdy basket or backpack for an al fresco light meal. Don't forget to stop on the way for some freshly baked breads and desserts—cupcakes, brownies, or cookies—that guests can easily serve themselves, without forks or plates.

Three Bean Salad with Tuna
Zaalouk Moroccan Ratatouille
Salpicón de Mariscos
Tapenade
Smoked Salmon Taramasalata
Bread and Dessert

MISSION ROSE GARDEN PICNIC

There are many places to picnic in Santa Barbara; among them are the Sunken Gardens at the Courthouse and my personal favorite, the Mission Rose Garden just across from the famed Santa Barbara Mission. There are benches to sit on or bring a blanket—it's so beautiful there surrounded by the roses. Sweet cheeses and nuts with a dessert wine provide just the right ending for viewing the Mission, with the majestic mountains in the background.

Falafel Chicken
Tehina Sauce
Shepherd's Salad
Pita Breads to make wraps
Assorted Cheeses, Nuts and Fresh Fruit
Cantuccini

ACKNOWLEDGEMENTS

I have written my second cookbook, passed out from joy, and woke up—from an incredible year full of growth, development and maturity. After assembling this new book, now needing to write my dedication, there are so many names to acknowledge that this turned out to be the most difficult part of this whole process. When thinking about names to include, I went through and thought of all who helped me get through it. This is a very personal choice and there is no wrong determination.

If I could literally recognize each and every person in my life from the beginning to this point in time, the list would have to start with my grandparents who established the influence of good food in my day-to day life; in particular Hilda, my father's mother, whom I watched and studied with respect and deep admiration. My parents, who supported my direction and achievements. All the cooks I have worked with over the last 30+ years, demonstrating the qualities I regarded and honored highly. Each and every facet of each and every event I have catered for the clients who put their trust in me and in my capabilities as an imaginative chef and party planner. Last but not least, a mountain of friends—I acknowledge you ALL, with many thanks and gratitude.

It is such an honor to work alongside the many gifted collaborators on this cookbook. Photographers Jess Roy and Karen Nedivi, recognizing the ease in which you both captured what I wanted to share, your attention to detail and creating images that jump off the pages.

Kamila Storr, my editor—your proofreading and editing greatly added to the readability of my work, and I appreciate you taking on this project with such passion and dedication. Welcome Constanza Di Gregorio! Thank you, mille grazie, muchas gracias, for your willingness, readiness and desire to jump in and create these beautiful pages. Local friend, lovely Nina Chesley and vegetarian chef Randy Graham, who were so willing and open to test some recipes and share your detailed comments. Danica Dahm and Giselle Soldati, thank you for assisting and helping create the shots for these pages.

Many thanks to the beautiful and talented Yasmina Ksikes for generously sharing your grandmother's Moroccan recipes. Sally Ruhl, I am very grateful to you for the thorough analysis of my manuscript. Cindy Kalmenson—OH ! how your garden grows—thank you for sharing your bounty. Kristina Kulik, I am so grateful for all the experiences and travels we will always look back on with joy and delight. "I could eat a little something". Best friends are those who keep giving, even when there is nothing to give in return. All my love. Adam Newman, thanks for the diversion from the norm. Always to be remembered, our journey through many countries, full of great food and experiences we shared on our travels together. Christie and Diana at Porch in Santa Barbara, thank you for welcoming me into your space and supporting my craft.

All of my current and past clients; in particular, thank you to Martha, Elisabeth, Anne, Bobbie, and Nancy, for being open and giving of your homes. All the stores, establishments and event planners for carrying and promoting my products in both Ojai and Santa Barbara and for supporting me as a local chef.

And finally...my daughter Chiya Bella, who has an amazing, discerning palate, and is always THE most honest person; you are a joy and the LOVE of my life.

Thank you all...from my heart!

About the author

Robin has made a career as a private chef providing home-cooked healthy foods using classic techniques honed at the Culinary Institute of America in New York. Raised in the Washington DC area, she ate her way through the city's most prominent restaurants at a young age. Her early exposure to fine dining with her food-loving family sparked her lifelong passion and love of cooking. Through travel and work abroad, she has developed her charming Mediterranean cooking style. Cooking and teaching locally in Ojai and Santa Barbara, Robin injects her style into recipes that have been featured during local events for many years. This success has led to publishing her first cookbook and development of "A Taste of Ojai" product line.

A *Taste of Santa Barbara, Crafting a Meal* imparts the flavors of the Mediterranean into these recipes, infusing lemon, rosemary, herbes de Provence, chilies and garlic into three distinct salts and seasoning blends. Robin lives in an oak-shaded neighborhood in the Ojai Valley, surrounded by nature and the scenic beauty of the local mountains Ojai is famed for.

Graphic Designer

Constanza Di Gregorio is a Graphic Designer and Sculptor who developed her art between Buenos Aires (Argentina) and Florence (Italy). She is now living in the Ojai Valley (California, USA), where she is constantly working on new projects. As an avid world traveler, her work experience at one of the most important publishing houses in Italy and her studies at the prestigious *Academy of Fine Arts of Florence* have greatly influenced her interest in designing books, especially those about cooking. "Words shorten distances", she often says, and this book is proof of how people can be closer to the fascinating world of culinary culture. To see more of her work, visit: www.constanzadigregorio.com

Photographers

Jess Roy is a creative artist who is drawn to authentic storytelling through natural light photography. She divides her time as a photographer, designer, stylist, and creative consultant and loves working with passionate people. Jess lives in Santa Barbara with her husband, Matthew, and daughter, Penelope, and enjoys the farmer's market, hunting for housewares, and cooking up a storm. To see more of her work, visit www.jess-roy.com.

Karen Nedivi is an Ojai based photographer and videographer. Collaborating with Robin brings together her passion for food and photography. To see more of her work, visit: handeyepictures.com

INDEX

Italicized page numbers with a *p* represent a photograph